Little Zoo by the Red Cedar

The Story of Potter Park Zoo

Kevin Hile

Strategic Book Publishing
New York, New York

Strategic Book Publishing
An imprint of AEG Publishing Group
845 Third Avenue, 6th Floor — #6016
New York, NY 10022
www.StrategicBookPublishing.com

ISBN: 978-1-60693-062-5
SKU: 1-60693-062-1

Printed in the United States of America

For Herman, Bingo, and Jim

Acknowledgments

The success of Potter Park Zoo is the result of the hard work of many, many people. Likewise, the success of this book has been the result of the contributions of more than just this one author. I wish to thank all those who have so generously given their time and resources for the sake of making this book the best it could be.

I wish to acknowledge, first of all, all those who agreed to interviews. Almost half the information contained within these pages comes from the staff and volunteers—past and present—who have been involved with the zoo. Some people I have quoted more than others, but this does not mean I value some of their memories and insights more than others. Much of the factual information I include comes from my lengthy conversations with them. Therefore, thank you Gerry Brady, Jan Brigham, Judi Corr, Jo and Dave Dickert, Maisie Downey, Doug Finley, Dr. Tara Myers Harrison, Jim Hough, Murdock Jemerson, Dennis Laidler, Ellen and Sonny Lumbert, Ina Martin, Tracy McMullen, Mary Anne McNamara, Diane McNeil, Jerry Miller, Eric Reickel, Dr. Jim Sikarskie, Bruce Snyder, Bill Swix, Dr. Duane Ullrey, Carol Webster, and Kelliann Whitney. I also wish to thank them for reviewing the draft of this book to help me verify and correct factual information.

Among the people listed above, an additional thanks to Mary Anne McNamara, for loaning me many articles about the zoo from her personal collection; Jan Brigham, who let me borrow valuable photos from the zoo keepers' collection and who spent considerable time answering additional questions I had; Bill Swix, who sent me his video of Tombi being trained, as well as other interesting materials;

Maisie Downey, who loaned me several photographs for scanning; and Diane McNeil, for loaning me the children's letters from her files. Additional letters from children were loaned to me by zoo docents Karl Zollner Jr., Jill Garnett (who also gave me the animal enrichment photos), and Junis Zumberg. I am also grateful to Susan Owens, who loaned me the photos of her kids on the zoo train. Melissa Ingells, daughter of the late *Lansing State Journal* photographer and columnist Norris Ingells, provided me with photos of Bingo's surgery; another former *Journal* photographer, Bruce Cornelius, provided me with the owl photograph; Mike Buda of *Michigan Country Lines* provided the photo of Jim Hough at a book signing. Many additional photographs were taken recently by zoo volunteer Bruce Bolender and by Constance Wardell—again, my thanks. My business partner, Jim Fordyce, provided several photos, too, including the author photo. Also, I am grateful to Judy Kish, who retired as office manager at the Society's office in 2006. Although I did not interview her, Judy helped me with additional fact checking and provided other background information. Teresa Masseau, office manager for the Potter Park Zoo, also assisted with fact checking.

Further gratitude goes to Clara Bratton, naturalist at the Fenner Nature Center, and April Honsowitz, an employee with the Department of Parks and Recreation, who pointed me to the nature center's archives and answered additional questions I had.

I did a lot of research for this book, but I also received much help during this process. Huge thanks and gratitude go to David Votta at the downtown Lansing branch of the Capital Area District Library. David did a lot of digging for resources that I could use, including books, City Council minutes, clippings, and old photographs stored in the library's history room. I picked David's brains a lot, trying to brainstorm possible resources I could draw on, and he answered my questions with great enthusiasm and interest in this project. Thanks, David!

Also, thank you to Potter Park Zoo Docent Association historian Joanne Harvey, and her fellow docent Eileen Agase, who gathered up all the newspaper clippings stored at the Society's office and arranged them chronologically. Thanks for saving me many, many hours of work!

Thanks go to my dear friend, Motoko Huthwaite, for proofreading the final manuscript one last time before this book went to the publisher.

Additional thanks to Jim Hough for writing the jacket blurb. Jim is very humble about his role in helping the zoo back in the days of the Friends, but his volunteer work and his many columns in the *Lansing State Journal* form the heart of this book. He is the "Jim" listed on the dedication page. As I wrote these pages, I could almost hear his voice urging me on to do it right, be fair, give credit where it was due, and preserve the memories of the past because they are the foundation for the future.

Last, but never ever least, to my wife, Janet, who is my first-run proofreader and should have been an editor herself, had she shown an interest in the field. Thank you for being so patient and understanding with me while I spent over a year putting this book together. You're the greatest!

Introduction

When I first visited Lansing's Potter Park Zoo in 1998, I viewed it through the biased eyes of a zoo snob. At the time, I was still living in Ferndale, Michigan, just a stone's throw away from the Detroit Zoo. I had been volunteering at Detroit as a docent (volunteer educator) for about three years at the time, and although I was preparing to move to the Lansing area for a new job and a new life, I was reticent to leave my work at a world-class zoo. The Detroit Zoo boasted a hundred-acre spread, including exhibits ranging from the historic building near the front of the zoo that housed the butterflies, exotic birds, and even an art gallery and movie theater, to the five-acre Great Apes of Harambee exhibit, a wonderful home for chimpanzees and lowland gorillas that had been dedicated by Jane Goodall herself.

I had learned from another docent at Detroit that Lansing had a zoo, too, so I decided to check it out and learn about volunteer opportunities there. My wife, Janet, and I arrived on a beautiful, sunny spring day. We turned off Pennsylvania Avenue onto the long access road that parallels the Red Cedar River as it leads visitors beneath a canopy of mature oak trees, past picnic areas, flocks of well-fed geese, a canoe rental business, and a flower garden. I was excited by the prospects of seeing a zoo in such a natural setting, as compared to the Detroit Zoo, which is hemmed in by a congested freeway and one of Detroit's busiest roads, Woodward Avenue.

A short stroll from the parking lot led to a small, cabin-like structure that was the admissions booth. After paying a small admission fee, we entered the zoo, where we were greeted by a charming penguin sign welcoming visitors. There was a camel exhibit, spider monkeys, and a barnyard near the front of the zoo, and a rather impressive

Feline/Primate House, including lions, tigers, and gorgeous colobus monkeys, one of my wife's favorites.

By the time we got to the back of the zoo, however, my zoo snobbery was kicking in. The Bird/Reptile House was obviously over fifty years old, and nearby was a grotto area with several smaller species, such as meerkats, that also looked very dated. Having bald eagles and vultures in what appeared to be wire grain silos also hinted that this zoo was sorely lacking in funds for exhibit upgrades. The penguin exhibit, however, was obviously newer, and a pond with swans and deer was a tranquil and enjoyable sight. Nevertheless, after leaving Potter Park, I resolved to commute to Detroit for my volunteer work (this was back when unleaded gas was still about $1.00 a gallon). But the commute proved too wearying, so I decided to give Potter Park Zoo a chance.

I contacted the Zoological Society and asked about volunteering, and a meeting was arranged with Ina Martin, a longtime volunteer who still runs the docent training class, and Education Director Kelliann Whitney. I took the fifty-hour course over several weekends, learning to my delight that, unlike at the Detroit Zoo, docents were given animal-handling lessons and allowed to take some live critters on educational outreaches. Graduating in 1999, I found that tours, too, were more fun at Potter Park Zoo. Because of its smaller size—nineteen acres—it was much easier to cover all the animals before the children you were teaching grew tired and cranky. This was very different from Detroit, where I could spend ten minutes just leading my tour group to the first exhibit.

I also learned how much Lansing residents love their zoo, and how much the staff and volunteers are dedicated to it. After a while, their enthusiasm inevitably rubbed off on me. Yes, Potter Park Zoo does have its problems—mostly stemming from a lack of adequate funding—but what it has achieved is remarkable, too—doubly so, considering the many challenges it has faced.

Over the years, Potter Park Zoo has experienced flood, public drunkenness, vandalism, lethal attacks on its animals, disease, heartbreaking deaths, and chronic financial threats to its continued operation. It has also known the joys of the many successful births of rare and endangered animals, the growth of an outstanding educational department that easily rivals that of any other zoo in the country, the benefits of a spirited community that has stepped in repeatedly to aid the zoo, and the support of veterinarians who have performed groundbreaking medical procedures benefiting the scientific community.

Despite all this, I still come across people in the mid-Michigan area who don't realize that Lansing has a zoo. Some of them, amazingly, have lived in Lansing or nearby for much of their lives. This degree of ignorance seems unfathomable to me. Of course, I'm an animal lover, and not all people are. Sadly, with most Americans now living in urban or suburban homes and the farm life receding into the past of our collective consciousness, America's connection to nature has been lost. But this makes zoos all the more important for us and our children, who may never otherwise get the chance to see a wild animal more exotic than a squirrel, a mouse, or a sparrow.

So, why write a history of Potter Park Zoo? Primarily, it is to honor the dedication and devotion of all those who have kept it alive and growing for nearly a century. It is because of their hard work and their faith that this little zoo by the Red Cedar River is a worthwhile place for people to experience and to learn from, and that it still exists today. By keeping the memory of Potter Park Zoo's past alive, I hope that the reader of this book will better appreciate how far it has come, how much has been achieved, and how much potential the future holds for Michigan's oldest zoological park.

Note for the Centennial Edition

As with any work of history, this book will become outdated within a year or two. It is my intention to continue researching and following the story of Potter Park Zoo for years to come. The zoo will celebrate its one hundredth year in 2020, and that landmark year will hopefully be commemorated with a special anniversary edition of *Little Zoo by the Red Cedar.*

In addition to updating the years from 2008 to 2020, I wish to go back and conduct further research on the zoo's early years, especially those years covering the 1920s through the early 1940s, for which I could find no one still alive who worked at the zoo at the time. If anyone reading this book has information available about Potter Park Zoo's early days, I would be most grateful if you contacted me through my publisher. Thank you.

Contents

1

The Early Years

In the heart of Lansing, Michigan, on a nineteen-acre plot of land at the eastern end of a bucolic, wooded park by the Red Cedar River, there is a zoo. Unless you happen to be familiar with it already, or seek it out on purpose because you love zoos and discovered it while surfing the Internet to plan a trip to the state's capital, you might very well miss it. Lacking the prominent water tower sign that graces the grounds of the Detroit Zoo (making it impossible to miss from the freeway) and without any billboards to draw attention to it, the only way a passerby will spot this particular zoo is if he or she notices the modest, yet colorful sign while driving along South Pennsylvania Avenue just south of I-496. In fact, there are many Lansing area residents who still don't know of its existence.

This is Potter Park Zoo. Opened to the public with a small collection of animals in 1920, it also happens to be Michigan's oldest operating zoological park, founded seven years before the next oldest Michigan zoo, the Detroit Zoo.

Today, Potter Park Zoo has over 400 animals, including numerous highly endangered species, as well as an impressive education department, and a growing role in research that includes groundbreaking work in animal medicine. It is an active participant in the worldwide zoo community's wildlife conservation goals.

But getting to this point has been a long and arduous road, and the course for the future of this little zoo remains in doubt. Visiting Potter

Park Zoo today, any guest might conclude that this popular park is a great success. Visited by over 350,000 adults and children each year, it is easily mid-Michigan's most popular family attraction.

Lansing's zoo, as we know it today, is vastly different from what it was through most of its history. How it has changed and grown is reflective of the evolution of many zoos across the United States, though Potter Park Zoo has perhaps struggled more than most.

How Lansing Got a Zoo

Back in the early twentieth century, people had a very different idea of what qualified as a zoo. The founders of the city, including such people as James M. Turner, Charles J. Davis, J. Henry Moores, and James W. Potter, made their fortunes from railroads and the vast supply of lumber in Michigan's sprawling woodlands. Even after the economic crash of 1893, when some of these men lost their fortunes, they were able to reestablish themselves as the area's forest industry barons. Along with such wealth, these early business leaders, several of whom would enter Lansing politics, bought large tracts of land. Some of them, too, put animals on their property, usually elk and deer, which roamed about freely. At the time, these were considered zoos of a sort, and there were several in Lansing by the 1910s. For example, Davis owned a herd of deer on his land, but also had several other animals, "including a pet otter whose favorite pastime was paddling up to the timber baron, upon his arrival from his downtown office, and begging to be slid across the ice of Davis' fish-pond," as historian Birt Darling related in his *City in the Forest: The Story of Lansing.*[1]

Early Zoos

The history of zoos goes back as far as 2300 BCE, when archeological records show that the city of Ur in Sumeria had a collection of exotic animals. Early zoos, more commonly thought of as menageries, were usually collections for the ancient world's wealthy rulers, including those of Egypt, Assyria, Rome, Macedonia, China's Zhou Dynasty, the Aztec Empire, and the Mogul emperors of India. During more recent centuries in Europe, rulers such as King Louis XIV of France and Ivan the Terrible, czar of Russia, kept menageries.

As kings lost power and republics were formed, such menageries were turned over increasingly to the general populace. Zoological gardens were established in the late-eighteenth century, and the influence of scientists such as Charles Darwin led to more academic curiosity about animals. The first modern age zoological park was the Regent's Park Zoo, established in London in 1828; the first in America was the Philadelphia Zoological Park, which opened in 1874. Not long after, in 1886, the National Zoo in Washington, D.C., was created, in part to preserve disappearing American wildlife such as the bison. Many other now-famous zoos, such as the Bronx Zoo, would be established in the years to follow, mostly along the East Coast. Michigan would wait until the 1920s for its first zoos, however.

Lansing was a growing city at the time, and was still in the process of establishing public services, one of the last of which was a parks system. In the early 1910s, there were two public parks in Lansing: Reasoner Park in the northern part of the city, and Belvedere Park, which was situated along the Grand River. The latter included eighteen acres of land donated by Moores in 1909, after whom the park was soon renamed. These two modest public lands were run, along with the cemeteries, by the Public Works Department. It was clear to the city's leaders, though, that there was opportunity for much more in the way of a parks system.

Mayor J. Gottlieb Reutter hired H. Lee Bancroft to be the city's forester and run the newly established Department of Parks and Cemeteries in 1914. Bancroft soon made a name for himself as a highly energetic and enthusiastic man who had a knack for getting well-to-do landowners to donate property to the city's parks system. One of these wealthy men was James W. Potter, a timberman after whom the city of Potterville southwest of Lansing is named. The Potters first made their money by owning a company that built wooden water sluices in California during the Gold Rush. Potter then moved his family to Michigan, where he continued making money in timber and construction. After arriving in Lansing, he purchased a large chunk of land east of what became Moores Park. According to Darling:

> The tract, originally known as the Morgan and Zabriski plot, had once extended from Mt. Hope avenue on the south to East St. Joseph street on the north, and from the Michigan Central Railroad tracks on the west as far east as a line extended from the center of Holmes street. When it was acquired by Potter in 1903 this entire region had only one farmhouse, and the private "zoo" of former Mayor Charles J. Davis adjoined it on the north.[2]

An undated photo of James W. Potter (photo courtesy Capital Area District Library/ Forest Park Library and Archive)

Potter was not a man known for his generosity, and so when he proposed donating to the city fifty-eight acres of his land adjacent to the Red Cedar River in 1912, some folks were a little surprised, though pleasantly so. Actually, Potter had ulterior motives. The land grant was part of a deal with the city. Potter wanted to develop the land nearby this donated tract, along with other investors, and at the time it was considered to be quite a distance from downtown. To bring people in, he proposed that the city extend its streetcar line from Michigan Avenue to Pennsylvania Avenue and the Mt. Hope cemetery; in exchange, he would donate the park land. When city commissioners, Mayor Reutter, Alderman Burt Baker, and Park Commissioner Harry P. Woodworth visited the park to learn what was there, they were stunned by what they saw: a property filled with stately oak trees and including twenty acres adjacent the river. It was a time when Americans were much less mobile than they are today, and many of these city leaders had not visited this wooded area—literally just a mile from downtown as the crow flies—since they were children. "I was not aware of its beauty …," said Woodworth. "I had not been there for years and had forgotten the place. I wished that all citizens of Lansing would visit the grounds and then they would understand what the city will lose should the proposition not go through."[3]

The city accepted Potter's proposal in June 1913, agreeing to the streetcar extension, as well as promising to make upgrades to nearby Dakin Street and a bridge. But the next year they told Potter that there was not enough money to extend the railway all the way to the cemetery. Refusing to seal the deal if the streetcar was not extended to Mt. Hope, Potter made a counter-offer, telling the city that if the Michigan United Traction (M.U.T.) Company, which had been contracted to do the work, needed more money, then he would loan an additional $2,500 at five percent interest. Potter also argued convincingly that the citizens of Lansing would not agree to $10,000 in planned improvements to the park should the streetcar not even reach the property (this was in addition to $25,000 that Potter and his wife, Sarah, gave the city to construct a pavilion). These improvements included canoe docks and flower gardens.

The land was regarded to be too valuable to allow it to slip away. The growing popularity of motor boating would find many fans of the recreational activity flocking to the park, as well as those who enjoyed canoeing. The park would also become a final link in a chain of parks that led from the gardens at Michigan Agricultural College (now Michigan State University) to parkland at Waverly Road. Plans were also made to build a spur track of the Grand Trunk Railroad next to the park so that people could visit it more easily. The financing was worked out, and Potter deeded the land to Lansing on the condition that it remain public land in perpetuity.

With the financing settled, Potter Park formally opened on July 5, 1915, with Potter making an appearance at the park to officially present the land to Mayor Reutter and Chamber of Commerce President W. K. Prudden. The event not only celebrated the gift of the park, but also the renewed vitality of Lansing after it had recovered from the 1893 depression. A "mass basket picnic" for all citizens was proposed by Judge Edward Cahill, according to Justin L. Kestenbaum in his *Out of the Wilderness: An Illustrated History of Greater Lansing,* and was enthusiastically supported by the mayor. About 25,000 people attended the event. "The plans for the picnic included a band concert, balloon ascension, a dedication ceremony, logrolling contests, and a gigantic tug-of-war between teams representing the 'north side,' as North Lansing came to be called, and the east side."[4] A story in the *Lansing State Journal* reported that, despite a chance of rain, the new streetcar line was packed, and car and truck traffic was also considerable.[5]

So it was that the new park along the Red Cedar was a big hit with Lansing, but there was no zoo there yet. The parkland increased by another twenty-seven acres when Potter donated additional land to the city, and in June 1921 a large pavilion was completed, thanks to more money given to the city by the Potters. Meanwhile, something interesting was happening back at Moores Park.

Bancroft, the parks director, had gotten James M. Turner to move his elk to Moores Park, and Charles J. Davis also transferred his deer there, thus creating a new zoo in 1915. In fact, one might say that Moores Park was Lansing's first real zoo, since it was the first to actually be managed by the city and not by a private animal collector. However, within a span of a few years, the animals followed their natural instincts, and soon there were too many deer and elk for the park to contain. In 1920, Bancroft decided to move them to the larger Potter Park. In addition to the deer and elk, two raccoons were donated to the new zoo, as well as a bear. The bear was presented to the city by a local boy scout troop that named the bruin General Pershing, in honor of John Joseph "Black Jack" Pershing, the man who led U.S. forces in Europe during World War I.

So it was that Potter Park Zoo was founded in 1920 with two raccoons, a bear, and herds of deer and elk. At the time, however, the zoo was not by any stretch of the imagination a separate entity from the park. It would be more accurate to say that, compared to today's standards, what Lansing had was a large public park with a few animals thrown in for interest. However, it was still considered a zoo, and thus became Michigan's first public zoological park.

LANDMARKS OF THE 1920S, '30S, AND '40S

Other than the pavilion, there was not a lot in the way of buildings in Potter Park. The only other structure to be found there, other than the canoe docks, was a small stone building on the east side of the park that was the former city dog pound (currently housing the keepers' office next to the rhino exhibit) that was incorporated into the zoo. The parkland continued to grow in 1927, when city resident Sophie Turner donated seventeen more acres to the park, thus bringing its size to the present-day 102 acres. The rest of the decade saw little else happen at the zoo as America enjoyed the Roaring Twenties, until the stock market crash of 1929 that sent the world into the Great Depression.

Deer were among the first animals exhibited at Potter Park (photo courtesy Capital Area District Library/Forest Park Library and Archive).

A postcard dated 1928 features the relaxing charms of the Red Cedar River and Potter Park. The park was a popular destination in the 1920s and 1930s for family picnics, canoeing, and strolls along the bank (photo courtesy Capital Area District Library/Forest Park Library and Archive).

The Depression years actually turned out to have some highlights for the zoo. In 1929, Lansing added a Department of Recreation (later to merge with the Department of Parks and Cemeteries to form the current Department of Parks and Recreation), which had a full-time

The oldest building at the zoo predates it. The keepers' lounge was originally the City of Lansing's dog pound. For decades after the zoo was established, keepers who tended to animals near the building were consequently nicknamed the Dog House Crew (photo by Kevin Hile).

director who could pay more attention to the zoo. A long-planned-for zoological building was completed late that year, as well, and is the structure that became the Bird House. Next, in 1930, the Lion House was completed during Herbert Hoover's administration. Interestingly, the exact same architectural plans were used to construct an exhibit building at the Toledo Zoo; that building has since been converted into the Carnivore Café. The original Lion House (now the Feline/Primate Building) became the central feature of Potter Park Zoo. In the manner of exhibit buildings of the day, however, it was a cold, cavernous affair, distinguished by its concrete floors, iron bars, and barren animal enclosures.

Old-Style Exhibits

People once knew very little about animals and their needs, even as recently as the early twentieth century, and this was reflected in how they housed wildlife in zoos at the time. Usually, whether an animal was social (like a gorilla) or solitary (such as a tiger) in its habits, they were all kept individually in their cages. They were not given anything more than food and water; they had no place to hide from people who were staring at them; and they

The current Bird/Reptile House was completed in 1929. In recent years many people have come to believe, erroneously, that the building was constructed by the Works Progress Administration, even though the WPA was not established until 1935. Today, the structure remains so sturdy that it doubles as a tornado shelter in times of inclement weather (photo courtesy Mary Anne McNamara).

The Feline/Primate Building (formerly the Lion House) was completed in 1930 and underwent a complete renovation in 1989 (photo by Kevin Hile).

An undated postcard shows lions in their outdoor exhibit at the zoo. Early zoo enclosures featured concrete and iron bars, and would be considered inhumane by today's standards (photo courtesy Capital Area District Library/Forest Park Library and Archive).

had nothing in their cages to stimulate their natural habits, such as hidden food, simulated boulders and trees, or the occasional toy, which are commonly put in enclosures today. This all meant that zoo visitors would see animal behavior that little resembled what they would do in the wild. Animals slept a lot, paced back and forth repetitively, and often sickened and died for no apparent reason. It would not be until the 1950s that this sort of treatment would start to change as people became more sympathetic toward zoo residents.

The next big improvement to the zoo came in 1936. Two years of planning had, with the help of President Franklin D. Roosevelt's Works Progress Administration (established in 1935), resulted in the creation of Monkey Island and the small moats area by the Bird House. Taking a cue from a similar baboon exhibit at the Detroit Zoo, parks director H. Lee Bancroft felt that a large rock island, surrounded by a moat, would make a great exhibit for the zoo, especially if it were populated by lively rhesus monkeys. In the mid-1930s, the Duck Pond exhibit that is located near the back of the zoo was also completed. Finally, just before the war, the zoo built its first aviary in 1941. The animal collection at Potter Park was fairly modest during the 1920s and '30s, though it slowly obtained more interesting animals, such as monkeys and an African lion named Pete, who lived at the zoo for twenty years before finally passing away in 1947.

The central core of Potter Park Zoo, including Monkey Island, was erected in 1936 by the WPA (photo courtesy Potter Park Zoo Society).

A postcard from 1942 shows visitors enjoying the monkey exhibit. Notice the exercise rings near the top for the rhesus monkeys to play on. (photo courtesy Capital Area District Library/Forest Park Library and Archive).

During World War II, money, of course, was in short supply as America spent all its available resources battling the Axis powers. This affected zoos across the country and the world, so that it was an achievement for zoos simply to maintain what they had. Potter Park Zoo managed to survive the lean times, however. During these rough years, the supervisor of Potter Park was Keith K. Kreag, who left Lansing in 1946 to become the first education curator at the Detroit Zoo. (Unfortunately, neither the City of Lansing nor the zoo maintains employee records dating back that far, so there is no documentation of Kreag's years at Potter Park Zoo). With Kreag's departure after the war, Bancroft was left with just himself and Assistant Forester Carl Fenner—who was hired in 1923 and after whom the Fenner Nature Center on Mt. Hope is named—to look after Potter Park. With a growing animal collection and a popular park to maintain, someone was sorely needed who could dedicate his or her time fully to these assets to the city.

THE TED DOWNEY YEARS

So it was that in 1946 Bancroft hired Theron "Ted" Downey to supervise Potter Park and its zoo. Downey's father, like so many early residents of mid-Michigan, had been involved in the lumber business, having been in charge of a lumber camp in Michigan's upper peninsula. Indeed, he had helped build the Bird House back in 1930. However, Downey, originally brought in to be a forester, was hesitant about managing a zoo because he knew nothing about them. Downey "told them he would give it a year's chance," recalled his widow, Maisie Downey, "and if it didn't work out he wanted them to promise that he would get his old job back. Well, we went through it. I mean, the first year was tough, but you learn a lot by your mistakes. Ted was able to get acquainted with some other zoo men, especially the ones in Detroit."[6]

It is fair to say that Potter Park Zoo was impoverished. Bancroft, apparently, was not serious about running a real zoo like Detroit's, but aimed only to have a park with some animals in it. The result was that, like the youngest child in a large, poor family, Lansing's zoo got all the hand-me-downs. Whenever another zoo like Detroit had a surplus of a certain species, they would approach Downey to see if he wanted these unwanted animals. Downey would weigh the cost of caring for such an animal, and then either accept or reject the offer based on that. For example, Potter Park was offered an elephant back in the late 1940s, but Downey knew his zoo could not afford to take care of it, so he declined. Smaller animals, such as monkeys and black bear, were a bit easier to manage and found their way to Lansing.

Many times, care for young animals came under the auspices of the Downeys. One of Maisie's fondest memories, in fact, was when they took in two orphaned bear cubs, and raised them in their home for four months.

> Some conservation men notified Ted that they found these two babies in a den and the mother had been shot.... They asked Ted if

Ted Downey, shown in 1973 after his retirement (photo courtesy Maisie Downey).

> he'd be willing to take them, and he said yes, but he didn't really have a place for them.... And so he said [to me] "Would you be willing to do it?" And I said, "Well, I'll try...." We had a cage in our dining room, and I would have to bottle feed them, and that was a job! Taking one out and trying to keep the other one in, and I had to wear long, thick leather gloves to feed them with. When I had to clean out the cage, I used to take them and put them in the bathtub and keep them in there. After a while they got so they knew how to do it themselves, and they'd run into the bathtub and get in the bath by themselves!

She also took care of a baby golden spider monkey that the mother refused to raise. This was the first animal she had to take care of, which she bravely did, though she had no prior animal experience. "Ted called me and asked if I would be willing to try and feed the baby. And I said, 'Gosh, what would I feed it? It's just so tiny!'" They ended up feeding it canned milk from a baby bottle. Later, they added cereal to the milk, spoon feeding it. The infant monkey could not be left alone, and so whenever the Downeys had to leave home, they put

Black bear cubs Yogi and Boo Boo enjoyed running into the Downeys' bathtub and asking for their bath. Other bears at the zoo would later also be named Yogi and Boo Boo, which is only confusing from a historical perspective (photo courtesy Maisie Downey).

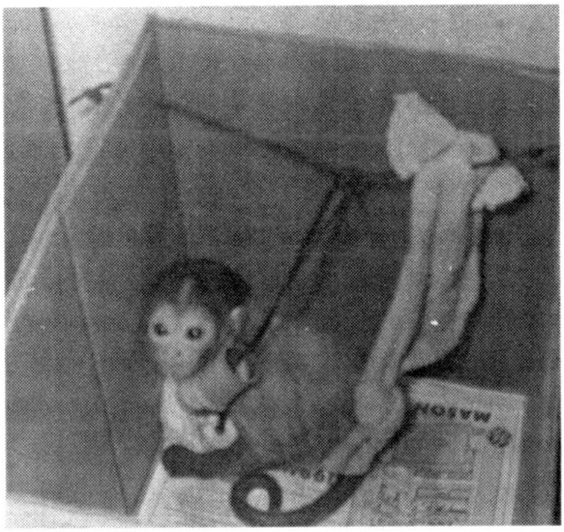

Maisie Downey also hand raised a golden spider monkey. It had to be fed so frequently that she and her husband took it with them whenever they would go out to a restaurant so that they could feed it on schedule (photo courtesy Maisie Downey).

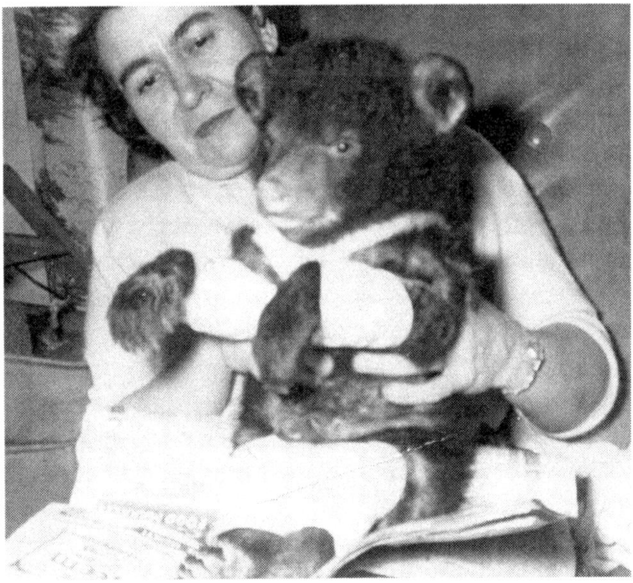

Maisie sometimes found herself taking care of sick animals, as well. This bear cub was born with a deformity called "swimmer's legs" that made it difficult for it to walk. Despite constant care, the poor bear did not survive long (photo courtesy Maisie Downey).

it in a carrier and took it with them. When it was older, there was no room at Potter Park for it, so it was sent to the Lincoln Park Zoo, where it stayed at the children's zoo. Unfortunately, the little monkey did not last long, contracting ringworm and dying soon after it was transferred.

In addition to begging and borrowing for animals, Ted Downey had to do the same for animal feed. Basically, as his widow recalled, the zoo had virtually no budget at all for animals or food. "A lot of times, Ted would have to go down and get day-old bread from the bakery and vegetables and things from the produce places because the city just didn't have that in their budget."

Without any formal training, Ted and Maisie had to wing it. They had no idea how to care for the animals for which Mr. Downey was held accountable. Fortunately, he came to know keepers and managers at other zoos well, and would often call them for guidance. He also took advantage of conferences where zoo directors and staff could go to learn from others in their business. Because Downey was uncomfortable with flying, he and his wife would only attend conferences within easy driving distance. The farthest they would go was Florida. "We did learn a lot from going to these conventions," reflected Mrs. Downey. "The first one we went to with Mr. Bancroft and his wife was in Kentucky. And we met Marlin Perkins [a wildlife expert famous for hosting the original *Mutual of Omaha's Wild Kingdom* on television], and Dr. Fisher of the Bronx Zoo."

Because there was so little money, Downey felt that, as with other zoos, a Zoo Society should be started that would be a nonprofit, fund-raising organization to help support Potter Park. However, Bancroft for some reason was dead set against the idea. Nor would he allow an admission fee to be put in place as a way of earning money to take care of the animals. Maisie Downey expressed that she was perplexed by this. Although Bancroft honestly believed that the zoo should be free to the public, which was certainly a kind motive, he extended little support for fund-raising initiatives that would take care of the animals in the manner they should be.

Downey himself was not well paid, and to help support his family, he and his wife opened a kennel, specializing in German shepherds, which they operated at the home they owned just south of the Arboretum on Mt. Hope. In addition to taking care of the zoo and park, Downey, in fact, also often assisted at the Arboretum, which is a story in itself.

THE ARBORETUM: LANSING'S FORGOTTEN ZOO

Now called the Fenner Nature Center, the Arboretum located on the south side of Mt. Hope near Aurelius Road was founded by Bancroft's assistant forester, Carl G. Fenner. Fenner was a renowned and beloved public figure in Lansing. The forester founded the Arboretum in 1959, and from that time until 1980, when it came under the supervision of its own naturalist, the Arboretum and Potter Park, under the guidance of Fenner and his employee Downey, operated much as if they were two branches of the same zoo.

Carl G. Fenner: Lansing's Great Forester

Carl G. Fenner graduated from a Lansing high school in 1917 and then attended Michigan Agricultural College for two years. Running out of money, he decided to raise funds for tuition by working for a tree surgeon and, later, as a coal miner. After finishing college, he was hired as an assistant forester by H. Lee Bancroft in 1923 because of his experience with the tree surgeon.

Fenner loved trees, and his first claim to fame was the result of ten years of work that began in 1939. He became interested in researching ways to save trees that had had their cambrian layers stripped off. This layer just beneath the bark of the tree circulates

Carl G. Fenner (photo courtesy Fenner Nature Center and the Lansing Department of Parks and Recreation).

sap, and when it is damaged severely by storms or other hazards, the tree dies. Some people had found that covering the exposed patch of tree with tar sometimes helped, but Fenner found this treatment unreliable. After years of research, during which he experimented with different mixtures to paste onto damaged trees, he became convinced that the key was simply to shade the exposed section of tree from the sun. Keeping the inner part of the tree from drying out helped the plant regenerate and survive. It was groundbreaking work in the forestry field.

Besides being a generous person whom Maisie Downey described as "a great man," Fenner's other claims to fame were running the city parks department from 1957 to 1962 after Bancroft retired, and founding the Arboretum on August 1, 1959. After he retired in 1962, the Arboretum was renamed the Carl G. Fenner Arboretum in his honor. Because of its focus on education and nature preservation, in 1994 it was renamed again as the Carl G. Fenner Nature Center.

Fenner was inducted into the Forestry Hall of Fame in 1976. Even after officially retiring, he kept active as a Sunday School teacher and also regularly educated children by leading nature walks and telling them about the local plants and animals that grace Michigan. He died on November 26, 1991.

The history of the Fenner Nature Center goes back to 1952, when Scott Turner, who was the grandson of one of the city of Lansing's founders and former mayor, James Turner, offered to sell a 126-acre parcel of his family's land along Mt. Hope Avenue to the city for $60,000. The beautiful tract of land had rolling hills, ponds, ten acres of swampland, and over 200,000 trees that had been cared for by the Turner family since the 1930s. The City, seeing an opportunity to add to its park system, purchased the land in November of 1952 and created Turner Park, which was renamed the Arboretum Park in August 1959, after the grounds had been remodeled under Fenner's direction to include over three-and-a-half miles of trails—later expanded to over five miles—and one building serving as a shelter. (In 1972, the "Avenue of Discovery" trail was also added, the first Braille nature trail for the sight-impaired to be built in Michigan.) Originally, the city planned to use the park simply for picnicking and playgrounds. Fenner, though, wanted to make more use of the park by turning it into a nature center. After the trails were completed, he devised a plan to create an American prairie exhibit. He procured three bison free from the federal government, while also seeking to add Texas longhorn steer and ponies.

The main building at the Fenner Nature Center (photo by Bruce Bolender courtesy of the Potter Park Zoo Society).

About ten acres within the park were reserved for the prairie exhibit and nature education area, while the rest of the 113 acres consisted of open land and trails offering opportunities to see Michigan's native wild birds, reptiles, amphibians, insects, and small mammals. By 1960, the park included 16 prairie dogs, three burrowing owls, a variety of ducks, Canada geese, four bison, three pronghorn antelope, and two Texas long-horned steer. The number of prairie dogs increased to twenty-five in 1963. There was also a "turtlearium," constructed in 1966, that held ten native Michigan turtles for easy public viewing.

By the early 1960s, word had gotten around that there was a nature exhibit in town, and people saw it as a resource where injured animals could be helped. The staff at the Arboretum thus found themselves caring for needy wildlife. For example, in 1962 they accepted twenty-one white-tailed deer fawns that had been taken out of the wild by well-meaning people who thought that these young deer were orphans. That may have been the case, though it was just as possible that they had been found while the fawns' mothers were hiding in the woods. In 1965, a snowy owl with a broken wing was found near the nature center and brought in to be cared for. Snowy owls were actually a fairly common sight that year because of a decline in the lemming population in the arctic at the time, the favorite food source for snowy owls. That year, too, a huntsman spider that had been found inside a bunch of bananas was brought to the center. The large spider, which is not a venomous species and has the admirable trait of eating cockroaches, had eggs with it. They soon hatched, and the Arboretum found itself with many many spiders! Other animals followed, including a naughty great-horned owl that had been raiding pigeon lofts in

1967, and an injured red-tailed hawk. An orphaned raccoon was so friendly with the staff that it became a kind of pet and mascot.

After the new Nature Science Building was dedicated on October 25, 1963, the Arboretum led the way in education long before Potter Park Zoo. Combining nature walks with animals they had at hand at the center, such as birds, frogs, and snakes, a thriving education program was built during the 1960s, and by 1969, with a staff of six led by Joan Brigham, the Arboretum was teaching over 11,000 children each year. In addition to teaching kids about wildlife, the Arboretum educated visitors about historic America. Every year, people could see demonstrations of maple sap harvesting for syrup in March, cider-making, and, more recently, the apple butter festival in October.

Brigham, who was hired as an assistant in 1966 and was head naturalist at the center from 1970 to 1982, expressed the education mission of the nature center well in a 1969 *Lansing State Journal* article: "Some of the kids are frightened of the ... woods at first.... When this happens we try just to show them what is here." She added, "And if they appreciate it they'll want to take care of it ... to do something about the pollution that is scarring the out of doors.[7]

Under the leadership of Fenner and Downey, Potter Park Zoo staff helped with the animals at the Arboretum, and both facilities drew on the medical assistance of the Michigan State University veterinarians. The Arboretum also proved to be a valuable source of food for the zoo's animals, many of which were fed on hay that was raised in a large field at the Arboretum. There was a close association between the two wildlife parks until 1980, according to Fenner Nature Center naturalist Clara Bratton, when the Parks and Recreation Department hired a dedicated manager for the Mt. Hope facility. However, even after that the zoo still often assisted with the animals until the last exhibit animal, Elvis the Bison, passed away in 2003. Maintaining wild animal collections for public viewing would become the job of the zoo, while Fenner Nature Center would focus on education and the enjoyment of native Michigan species that already called the woods and ponds there home.

THE ANIMAL COLLECTION: 1950S TO THE EARLY 1960S

Obtaining animals from other zoos, and occasionally from the wilds nearby, such as with the two adopted bears, Ted Downey managed to gather a respectable display of wildlife, including, at various times, two wolverines, a tapir, peacocks, four coatimundis, three porcupines, two zebus (also known as Brahma bulls), two zebras, two river otters, two wolves, two Canadian lynx, two bobcats, rheas, an ocelot, an anteater, bear cubs, a red kangaroo, a grey kangaroo, and the mainstay of the zoo, elk, deer, and bison. By the 1950s, in fact, the zoo had an impressive array of monkey species, including rhesus, spider, ringtail, and African green monkeys. The golden spider monkeys, which were given the reign of Monkey Island at what was then the center of the zoo, were amazingly popular with crowds. The spider monkeys replaced the rhesus monkeys on the island because the latter, as it turned out, were able to jump out of the enclosure, while spider monkeys are not quite as athletic. The island was equipped with a bare tree and even a kind of swing set and ropes for them to practice their climbing skills. Some less familiar species at Potter Park at the time also included over a dozen coypus (a type of South American rodent) and whydahs, which are small weaverbirds from Africa.

The co-monarch of Potter Park at the time was Duke the lion, the successor of previous king Pete, though Duke had to share his reign

The old bison and tapir exhibits (photo courtesy Capital Area District Library/Forest Park Library and Archive).

with Tony the tiger. Duke had the last laugh on Tony, however, when he was given a mate, Susie, and Tony remained a bachelor.

The zoo even had tigers back in the 1940s. Bobo the Bengal tiger was there many years before passing away from old age in 1949; then, in 1951, the zoo received Millie the Bengal tiger from Chicago's Brookfield Zoo. Poor Millie was none too happy with the transfer, however, as she had become very attached to her Brookfield keeper, Robert Bean. "Mr. Bean wept as zoo men crated the animal to be brought to Lansing," reported a *Lansing State Journal* article.[8] After spending two days getting the tigress into the cage in Chicago, it took nearly as much convincing to get her out. Spraying her with water, offering food, prodding her with sticks (which she chewed up) did not work; none of it worked until she finally became too tired to argue anymore and left the cage voluntarily. Thankfully, Millie did adjust to Potter Park Zoo and became a highlight of the park.

By the early 1950s, the park was setting attendance records, sometimes attracting as many as 300 visitors over the weekend; almost 200,000 people came by to see the animals in 1952. According to a *Lansing State Journal* article, in 1952 the zoo had "138 animals and 267 birds,"[9] by which, of course, the unnamed reporter meant *mammals* and birds, since birds are animals. The first pony rides were also offered in the 1950s through concessionaire Clifford Brailey, who provided them in the summer months to young zoo guests.

Ted Downey had proven himself adept at acquiring animals; many still came from other zoos as surplus, but some were also being ordered from animal suppliers, who obtained them from their native lands in Africa, India, and other points abroad. In 1953, Downey added coyotes as a new exhibit, and soon the zoo also saw the addition of timber wolves, Arizona the female mountain lion, and Jo-Jo the Guinea baboon. Jo-Jo, who was born at the zoo, became known as quite the imp. As a baby, he was an escape artist. Too small for the crude steel bars to contain him, Jo-Jo easily slipped out between the iron barriers to visit zoo guests face to face. He always returned to his cage, though, where his parents would reprimand him with a quick cuff.

HERMAN

Of all the animals at Potter Park Zoo, and perhaps all of Lansing, the most famous and special of all was Herman the Mexican burro. A common burro seems an unlikely candidate for most popular attraction at a zoo, but Herman was a true personality. Even the story of how he arrived at Lansing's zoo is remarkable. He was born in 1948, thousands of feet up in the sky, as his mother was being transported by plane from her homeland south of the border to America, where she had been sold to the Shrine Circus. Once in the United States, and after he had grown up a little, Herman was sold to Henry L. Owens, who turned him into a band mascot for the Shriners. After a couple years of life in the entertainment industry, Herman was sold to Potter Park Zoo in 1951.

Once at the zoo, Herman, a rather attractive burro with his white, shaggy fur coat, became instantly popular with children and adults alike. Perhaps recalling his showmanship days with the Shriners, Herman had a way of endearing himself to people. He exhibited great enthusiasm for carrots and sugar cubes that people gave him, and also loved a good scratch behind the ears. Sometimes rather insistent about it, Herman would nudge and nip at people who ignored him. He adored being the center of attention! He was quite intelligent, too, often fooling the keepers by managing to open his gate, then running back inside and pretending he had been there all along. He had a very loud bray that could carry for miles, and the neighborhoods surrounding the zoo could always tell when the burro was feeling spunky or stubborn.

Herman was called the "patriarch of Lansing's animal kingdom"—a title I'm sure Duke would have objected to—and was visited by local city mayors and other politicians for photo opportunities. When Ted Downey decided to leave the zoo in 1965, he made certain that he bade Herman a tearful farewell. Downey decided to leave because, as his widow explained, he had grown weary of battles with his superiors on how to run the zoo. He would move on to a job as manager of the MSU veterinary clinic, where he was later named an honorary vet for his work there. Downey had other jobs at MSU, too, before passing away in 1987.

As for Herman, his fate would be to play one of the most important roles in Potter Park Zoo's history.

2

A Friend in Need: Founding the Friends of the Zoo

Take an aging Mexican burro, a broken air circulation blower, a Hall of Fame journalist, and a civic-minded meter reader and you have the ingredients for the recipe that dramatically changed the course of Potter Park Zoo's history.

For over four decades, the zoo had basked in a peaceful, relatively uneventful existence. Though there were certainly challenges, especially budgetary ones, the modest zoo on the east end of Potter Park was, for the citizens of Lansing and its surrounding communities, a pleasant bonus feature to a relaxing setting. Here, people could come and see a lion, bear, or elk, while strolling through the grounds and burning off the calories of that afternoon's chicken sandwich and watermelon.

By the late 1960s, however, the zoo was beginning to show some age. The Bird House, Monkey Island, and the Feline/Primate House were all in need of repair. Less noticeable—but no less important—the zoo's infrastructure, including plumbing, sewer drains, and electrical wiring, were all decaying and in some cases no longer complied with building inspection codes. There had been an effort to pass a city millage in the early 1960s to provide additional money for improvements to the zoo, but it had failed.

The noticeable wear and tear was coming at a time when attitudes about zoos were changing. People were coming to understand that animals were not just brainless creatures to be caged for public entertainment. It was no longer considered enough to only provide these creatures with food, water, and a cage to sleep in; animals, just like people, needed stimulating and enriching environments that mimicked their natural homes. This increasing sympathy for animals was due to several important developments in the country at the time, including the dramatic changes in the social climate in America, which included more environmental awareness and a corresponding increase in empathy for animals as living, breathing beings with whom we share the planet. Some of this change can be attributed to the work of famous field biologist and chimpanzee expert Jane Goodall, who helped people become aware of the intelligence and emotions that animals can possess. Also coming into play was the revolutionary work of Dr. Heine Hediger. A former director of Switzerland's Basel and Zurich zoos, Hediger designed groundbreaking exhibits that closely simulated animals' natural habitats, thus making them much more humane places to live. Many zoos around the country, including the Detroit Zoo, were using Hediger's designs in their new exhibits.

In reaction to all this, the U.S. government was beginning to crack down on zoos that were operating on a sub-par level that was seen as inhumane to animals. Much of this attention was being put on what are typically referred to as "roadside zoos." Roadside zoos are privately owned wildlife collections operated by people who charge fees to visitors to see what is essentially a menagerie of exotic pets kept within chain link fences or other inappropriate enclosures.

As a city-owned facility, Potter Park Zoo had long been open to regular inspections by the U.S. Department of Agriculture (USDA), from which it received licensing to continue its operations. In 1969, as inspection time from the USDA came again, a ventilation blower had broken down in the Feline/Primate House. The result was that the air was growing quite pungent, even to the extent that it could be unhealthy for the animals inside. As a result of this, federal veterinarians evaluating the zoo recommended closing the building, at least until the problem could be fixed.

The general public in Lansing, already aware that the buildings and exhibits at their zoo were in a state of decline, took notice and began

Zoo exhibits, such as the old lion exhibit at Potter Park Zoo, used to be prison-like in many ways. Today, zoos try to mimic natural environments as closely as possible (photo courtesy Capital Area District Library/Forest Park Library and Archive).

to grow concerned that the zoo itself could close. Rumors were circulating that Lansing City Council members were considering shutting the zoo's gates for good. One person, Fred Rowe, a meter reader for the Board of Water and Light, took it upon himself to do something and make people aware of what he felt was an impending crisis at the zoo. He visited the desk of *Lansing State Journal* reporter Jim Hough, who already had a reputation as a cheerleader for the zoo after writing many supportive articles in his column, "The Onlooker." Hough was the obvious person to approach. The reporter recalled:

> Fred Rowe came in one day to my desk, and he didn't know me, and I didn't know him, and he started telling me all about Potter Park. How much it meant to him. And he felt bad that there was so much movement to close it. All this was kind of behind the scenes. This was mainly City Hall talk. So Fred said, "Jim, I've read your column forever, and I just think that you ought to look into this because if we have to give up Potter Park," he said, "we shouldn't do it without knowing how much the community is behind it." So I said, "Okay,

that's a fair enough thing." So I went down to the park, and I went into Herman the Mexican Burro's cage.... Frank Mainville was a photographer at the *Lansing State Journal* in those days. He followed me down there and took a picture of me interviewing Herman. When I came back, I wrote a column, and Herman's comment was, "Before we close Potter Park Zoo, maybe we should find out how many people would like to leave it open." And Herman called for a meeting. Herman thought that a Friends of the Zoo might be what Potter Park needed."[1]

Jim Hough at one of his book signings (photo courtesy Mike Buda, *Michigan Country Lines*).

Jim Hough

Inducted to the Michigan Journalism Hall of Fame in 2000, Jim Hough (pronounced "How") wrote for the *Lansing State Journal* from 1962 to 1988. He was a 1958 graduate of Central Michigan University, where he was among the first class to complete the university's then-new journalism program. CMU also inducted him into its Hall of Fame in 2003. Over the years, Hough wrote over 8,000 articles for his "The Onlooker" column, a regular human interest feature for the *Journal* that spoke on items of community interest and helped give readers a voice on events in the news.

Of all the columns Hough wrote, however, he is best remembered for those featuring Potter Park Zoo, about which he editorialized so often that his bosses sometimes had to specifically ask him to write about something else for a change. Several of his zoo stories, not just the one that helped start the Friends, were interviews with Herman, and for several years Hough served as Herman's voice. For his pivotal role in co-founding the Friends of the Zoo and for repeatedly serving as the zoo's champion in the public eye, some have regarded Hough as the "Founder of the Zoo in Lansing." This appellation was indicative of how many people felt that the establishment of the Friends of the Zoo marked Potter Park's initial transition from animal park into a more modern zoo. Hough, however, has said that there were too many people involved to give just one person the credit.

Two weeks after the column was published, a meeting was organized in the basement lounge at the *Journal*'s office. To Jim and Fred's delight, about 300 people showed up at the meeting, including Lansing's mayor, community leaders, reporters, and other citizens showing their support for Potter Park. The Friends of the Zoo was formed that night, and by September of 1969 it had almost 400 members. This increased to 1,500 members by March 1970 and reached 2,000 people by the end of that year.

WHOSE IDEA WAS IT, REALLY?

The reader may recall that Ted Downey had long ago proposed the formation of a zoo society, which his boss, H. Lee Bancroft, rejected. The idea remained comatose until 1969. Interestingly, when one talks to Jerry Miller, Downey's successor, and his assistant, Bill Swix, a rather different version comes out as to how the Friends of the Zoo got started. According to both of them, the zoo was never under any threat of being closed, at least not by the USDA. Swix commented:

> Jim Hough kind of remembers it a little differently. Actually, what happened was that we had blowers in the Lion House that circulated the air, and the motors burned out on the blowers, so we didn't have any circulation. So the Lion House really smelled bad. We were being inspected by the U.S. Department of Agriculture, and we were kind of buddies with the vet who was there, and he said we really needed to do something about that because people are really complaining bad. So the vet said, "Well, I can write you guys up, and they [the city of Lansing] will have to do something or close that building." Actually what they were going to do was close the Lion House down, not the whole zoo. That made them [the city] do something for the air quality in the zoo and the Lion House.[2]

Emphasizing that there was never any danger or maltreatment to the animals at the zoo, Miller agreed with Swix: "I don't recall them saying they were ever going to close us or anything. The USDA used to give us an inspection every so often, and of course we'd have some minor things, but I don't recall them ever finding anything so out of whack that they threatened to close us."[3] Hough, on the other hand, has maintained that the government veterinarians "were wanting to close the zoo" and that, at the time, it "was just a crummy place" because "there was nothing very natural in the habitat" for the animals.

Swix went even further to state that the concept of a zoo society actually sprang from his and Miller's minds. "We had already been working with Jim [Hough] and Art Mauk [who would become the first president of the Friends of the Zoo] to try to get this thing started because we needed some extra help in order to try to get the zoo growing."

The concept of a zoo society was not originated at Potter Park, of course, so no one in Lansing could make that claim. It was an idea borrowed from other zoos. As for the extent of the zoo's peril and whether or not it was actually at the edge of becoming defunct, that has become a matter of opinion. It is certainly possible that, as a professional journalist, Hough became privy to information about what was going on in Lansing City Hall that neither Miller nor Swix were party to, including possible plans to save budget money and close the zoo, rather than spend more to fix its problems. But as future zoo director Doug Finley would later pointedly remark in retrospect, "For Jim Hough to have to come and interview Herman ... and to have to say to the city that you have a zoo out here indicates that ... when the press has to tell us what to do then we're not doing a very good job ourselves, and the city wasn't doing a good job, or Jim Hough would never have seen the need to go out there and do that."[4]

Whatever the case might have been, though, all parties agreed that Potter Park Zoo needed some friends, and there is likewise no doubt that it was Hough's *Lansing State Journal* interview with Herman that served as the spark to light a flame that has been burning ever since. The people of Lansing heard the bray of the Mexican burro, and they came to the aid of Potter Park Zoo.

HERMAN THE MASCOT

Whoever first came up with the concept for the Friends of the Zoo is not nearly as important as the fact that it was, indeed, founded in 1969. Swix gave due credit to Jim Hough for getting the first meeting organized. Actually, when all is said and done, perhaps the true founder of the Friends was Herman. Everyone who visited Potter Park loved that old burro and would have been sorry to see him go had the zoo closed. Herman was recognized for doing his part when he was made the official mascot of the new Friends of the Zoo, and his image appeared prominently on their official logo.

Sadly, shortly after the zoo society was organized, Herman passed away in 1971. He had called Potter Park his home for twenty-three years. News of Herman's death struck a strong chord in the community, even surpassing the death of a very well known politician. Jim Hough recalled: "I wrote an obituary on Herman when he died, and it covered the entire upper section of the front page of the *Lansing State Journal*. On the third page inside the *State Journal* was the announcement of the death of Tom Dewey." Dewey was the former Republican New York governor who unsuccessfully ran against Harry S Truman in the 1948 Presidential election, though the *Chicago Tribune* famously printed the erroneous headline "Dewey Defeats Truman" the day after the election. "Herman was big stuff," Hough continued. "Kids all over town were crying about Herman."

Herman was the inspiration for the original Friends of the Zoo logo (courtesy Ellen and Sonny Lumbert).

"Our Dear Friend Herman"*

by Ellen Lumbert

Our dear friend Herman
Has now passed away
With him goes our love
Which grew more each day.

He left us with memories
many and fine,
Herman so gentle,
So sweet and kind.

His twinkling eyes that
Shone in the night
His vibrant bray saying,
"Give me a bite!"

A scratch on the ears,
A pat on the head,
A big juicy carrot,
An apple bright red.

So many hands that
Reached out to touch
These were the things
He cared for so much.

With tears in our eyes
We bid him so long,
But his memories remain
Ever on, ever on....

*Reprinted with permission from Ellen Lumbert.

It had been a long and good life, though. As Herman himself told Hough: "My ears have been scratched by a million kids, I guess. Some of those who scratched my head when they were little tots are now grown up and have children of their own. How many old donkeys are there in the world who have made so many children so happy?"[5] The zoo soon bought a new Mexican burro named Shawnee, and later another one, Hermina, became a resident. But although they were both loved, no one could ever replace Herman. A special memorial service was held by the Friends in Herman's honor, and his memory lived on for many years.

THE FRIENDS GET BUSY

The Friends of the Zoo quickly got organized for the tough job ahead. Arthur "Art" A. Mauk, a crime scene photographer for the

This photo of Ellen Lumbert with Herman is her favorite. Volunteers and staff were not supposed to give Herman treats such as carrots and sugar cubes, but they inevitably fell sway to his charms (photo courtesy Ellen and Sonny Lumbert).

Michigan State Police who was one of the Friends' cofounders, was elected the first president. The Friends knew that they did not have much time to prove themselves. Many newly created charitable organizations are dissolved within one or two years if they can't become established, viable entities, so the Friends had to quickly rally the community and solicit donations from area businesses. Mauk and Hough were granted time off from their police department and newspaper jobs, respectively, and made the rounds, asking for donations from area businesses.

One of the most generous donors, it turned out, was the publisher of the *State Journal* at the time, Louis A. Weil, Jr., whom Hough described as "a pretty cool guy." A hands-off publisher who liked to give his reporters as much freedom as possible and rarely visited the newsroom, Weil made a point to stop by Hough's desk one day. "He sat down at my desk," recalled Hough, "and he said, 'Jim, I like what you're doing with Herman and the Friends of the Zoo … I want to do several things…." Weil invited all the big area businesses, including General Motors, Motor Wheel, and Karl Story's Oldsmobile dealership, to Dines Restaurant on East Michigan Avenue. Here, Hough and Jerry Miller made a slide show presentation, featuring photos by *State Journal* photographer Bruce Cornelius, and made their plea. After the meeting, Weil bade farewell to each person at the door and said they would soon have someone (Hough or other Friends members) come to their business asking for a pledge of help to the zoo. Weil himself then made a generous personal donation of $20,000.

Money started to come in, and by September 1969, the Friends made their first gift to Potter Park Zoo: a pair of male aoudads (these African mountain sheep, also known as Barbary sheep, were later named "Rhonda" and "Rocky") that were purchased from the Detroit Zoo for $300. Early the next year, the organization bought a squeeze cage (a type of containment cage used to restrain large animals so they can receive medical treatment) for $269. The first big project would soon follow.

A Children's Zoo

One constant that has not changed since Potter Park Zoo was founded is that children are its biggest fans. It was unsurprising, then, that the first construction project that the Friends of the Zoo championed was a children's zoo. The goal, as Jim Hough wrote in a *Lansing*

State Journal article, was to raise funds "to complete what … will be the best children's zoo in the Midwest."[6]

Estimating the cost of construction to be about $300,000, the concept involved building an entirely separate zoo adjacent to the existing one. The Friends started a membership drive to bring in funds; they also initiated other money-earning projects, including a charity softball tournament and a button sale. The buttons proved extremely popular with the public, becoming collector's items that are now difficult to find. Of course, a bigger source of income came from private businesses and corporate donations, including a $10,000 gift from General Motors and $7,000 from car dealer Karl Story, but even with these gifts the project had to be divided into four phases. Eventually, the grandiose plans, including a 2,400-square-foot building, proved too ambitious, despite the enthusiasm of the Friends membership. In addition, city parks staff had researched other zoos around the country, concluding that separating the two zoos might actually cause attendance to the older zoo to decline.

So, in October 1971, the children's zoo plan was extensively revised. Instead of creating a completely separate children's zoo, some of the planned features would be incorporated into the rest of the main grounds. These included a revitalized barnyard area and a free-roaming petting zoo, where kids could feed some of the animals by hand.

Bill Swix (left) and Jerry Miller (photo courtesy Potter Park Zoo).

Jerry Miller and Bill Swix

After the departure of Ted Downey in 1965, Potter Park Zoo was run for many years by the dynamic duo of Gerald "Jerry" Miller and his assistant, Bill Swix. Miller joined the zoo in 1959 as a keeper, and was promoted to Zoo Manager when Downey left. Swix, who started working for the City when he was seventeen, had been an employee in Lansing's Field Office, where he worked in landscaping and maintenance, beginning in 1954. He spent six years as a zoo keeper, half a year as maintenance group leader for Fenner Arboretum, and six months as head zoo keeper before being named assistant zoo manager. Miller's duties included everything from managing the budget, record keeping to remain in compliance with federal and state laws, ordering and trading animals in the collection, public relations, and general cheerleading for the zoo. Since such responsibilities at a zoo continue 24-7 all year long, Swix was there as a backup whenever Miller was unavailable, as well as serving as Miller's partner in all the managerial duties. He was also, as coordinator of the Elephant Committee, in charge of elephant care and training.

THE FRIENDS CHANGE LEADERSHIP

Friends President Art Mauk stepped down from his office in 1971, later retiring from the police department and moving out of the Lansing area to settle in western Michigan. In his place, society cofounder Fred Rowe took over for the next year; he was followed by Denise Bancroft. All these people helped lead the Friends over the bumpy, nascent years. Jim Hough's worries over whether the Friends would survive the first couple of years were eased, and the group began to establish itself as a permanent fixture at Potter Park Zoo. The mood of concern over the future of Lansing's zoo and rumors of its closure were replaced by feelings of optimism and community spirit, both among the zoo's staff and among Potter Park's visitors.

The longest-serving president—and the woman whose name would most often be associated with leading the Friends of the Zoo—was Ellen Lumbert. Having been a member of the board of directors since 1969, Ellen became president in 1974 and headed the society until she stepped down in 1986. Her husband, Francis, better known as "Sonny," would also be very active in the Friends and would be its business manager for many years.

The years of Ellen's tenure as Friends president would see many changes at the zoo. As the head of the zoo's fund-raising organization, however, she had no unrealistic expectations for Potter Park. The zoo was limited by what it could aspire to, she realized, having only modest funding from the city. It would likely never be the equal of such parks as the Detroit or Cincinnati zoos, she felt. This did not mean, though, that the Lumberts and the Friends were without their aspirations.

"Initially," said Sonny, "we were formed just to make improvements in the zoo, not to expand it or bring in new animals. We wanted to make it a decent place for the animals to live in. The zoo had zoo keepers who were very dedicated to the animals, but our goal was to try to make it better for the zoo, the animals, and the zoo keepers."[7]

At the time the zoo society was formed, for example, the keepers did not even have standard uniforms. One of the early projects for the Friends during its first five years of operation, therefore, was to raise money and pay for keeper uniforms to bring more of an air of professionalism to the staff. Furthermore, there was no money in the city budget to offer ongoing zoo keeper training. The Friends responded here, too, by paying to send keepers to seminars and conferences so that they could offer improved animal care based on the latest research and the experiences of their colleagues. Even before the

Ellen Lumbert (photo courtesy Ellen and Sonny Lumbert).

Sonny Lumbert (photo courtesy Ellen and Sonny Lumbert).

society could think of raising funds for exhibit improvements, therefore, there was considerable groundwork to be done.

Getting the basics accomplished was difficult, however. In early 1974, when Ellen Lumbert was still secretary of the Friends and had not yet been elected president, the initial excitement of the Friends' founding had waned alarmingly. After those who had hopped on the bandwagon had disembarked because the early thrills had been replaced by hard work, only the true diehards remained. Membership declined from an early high of about 2,000 dues-paying people to below 500. The Friends of the Zoo also found itself butting heads with Lansing City Council members. According to *Lansing State Journal* reporter John Teare, "Hints of policy differences … appear to have dogged relations between the city administration and the Friends of the Zoo."[8]

Among the arguments was whether to accept an offer by Associated Builders and Contractors (ABC) to donate labor and materials for construction at the zoo, a proposal the city resisted because ABC used non-union labor. At the same time, city leaders were also proposing grand plans for the zoo, including expanding its grounds eastward across the Red Cedar River and into Crego Park; to pay for the expansion, Doug Finley, who was then assistant director under Theodore J. Haskell at the Department of Parks and Recreation, urged a millage be passed. However, it was suggested that the Friends be the organization to promote the millage, while Friends leaders felt this was a job for the city to manage, not a private organization.

Meanwhile, Lansing's Mayor Gerald W. Graves was making grandiose statements that he would make a bid for the zoo to be the home of the giant pandas that China had agreed to loan to the United States in 1972. This, while at the same time he was attempting to slash $7,000 from the zoo's budget. Fortunately, the City Council rejected such self-defeating cuts.

While city government made "only token appropriations for improvements" to the zoo, as Jim Hough noted in one of his columns,[9] ideas such as major expansions in acreage and obtaining animals of international importance were about as likely to happen at Potter Park as an all-beef chili competition hosted by PETA. In retrospect, much of this talk was likely just political grandstanding. The leaders of the society were much more concerned with rather practical issues, such as updating the air conditioning system for the forty-year-old lion house and improving the black bear exhibits.

FUND-RAISING EFFORTS GET CREATIVE

When Ellen Lumbert was elected president of the Friends, her main focus was establishing and maintaining a variety of creative fund-raising efforts to meet the organization's goals for the zoo. Among the activities the Friends created were a hole-in-one golf contest, a Fourth of July softball tournament in which the mayor's office staff competed against radio station and newspaper employees, and a celebrity auction broadcast on WJIM radio in 1977. Donations included prizes from area businesses, as well as some unique items, such as a drawing from the famous movie director Alfred Hitchcock.

Some events were specifically designed more to bring people to the zoo, rather than raise money directly. The Friends organized Potter Park Zoo's first Halloween celebrations, and in early December an "Open House" event was held featuring Santa Claus and refreshments. The Open House was begun in 1975 and would be the precursor to the modern, multi-week Wonderland of Lights holiday event, which was introduced in 1993 and welcomed 40,000 guests during its debut. Another event during the summer months was "Clown Days," a crowd pleaser for young and old alike during which professional clowns were invited to compete and perform in various categories at the zoo. Caught up in the increasing activity at Potter Park, the city got into the act as well, and, for several years during the 1970s, summer concerts featuring big band music drew crowds.

Thanks to the efforts of the Friends of the Zoo, by the summer of 1976, the mood at Potter Park had turned around 180 degrees. Just a few years earlier, people were wondering whether it would be best if the zoo's gates closed forever. Now, there was a revived spirit and excitement. Almost half a million visitors were coming to the zoo annually, according to an article by Hough, who quoted Jerry Miller as saying, "Our attendance has more than doubled since 1969, when the Zoo Society was formed."[10]

There would be more challenges to come in Potter Park Zoo's future, but a landmark corner had been turned. Finances, of course, were still a constant struggle for Ellen Lumbert and the Friends. It helped when more money came into the organization's coffers when the Friends took over operation of the zoo's pony rides, as well as concessions. Sonny became the business manager, handling the

Clown Days was one of the early fund raising events at the zoo. Here, Bingo the elephant poses for a postcard picture with a clown riding her. Normally, the keepers did not allow Bingo to be ridden; this was a rare exception (photo courtesy Capital Area District Library/Forest Park Library and Archive).

money from these various sources. "Then we had more money to do things with," recalled Sonny. "Ellen kept it percolating for years when it was sort of touch and go, but eventually we got over that hump—the transition between the original excitement and the point where we moved on to bigger and better things."

Exciting things were happening at Potter Park Zoo in the 1970s: new animals, new exhibits, and a community that stepped in to make it all happen. No longer just a place in the back of the picnic area of the park where visitors could see some exotic beasts, Potter Park was making its way down the winding path toward a modern zoo.

3

Community Spirit: Exciting Days at Potter Park

With the Friends of the Zoo establishing a firm toehold at Potter Park, the zoo was abuzz with ideas for improvements and new animals. It seemed as if everyone in the Lansing community wanted to pitch in, almost as if they had become aware for the first time that they had a zoo in their midst. While the first animal gift presented to the zoo by the Friends was the aoudads, the public had the winning vote on the next big purchase: an elephant.

The outcry for an elephant was so overwhelmingly insistent, in fact, that the Friends could not help but listen. Potter Park had never had an elephant before because of the expense, but it was going to get one now. The zoo and Friends worked together to decide on the purchase of a baby Indian (or Asian) elephant. At the time, such animals were still being shipped in from other countries (today, most exhibit animals are born in zoos). The cost of a baby elephant from Asia would be $3,500; in addition, actually shipping a live pachyderm from overseas would bring the total cost to the zoo to over $6,000 (remember, this was back in 1972, when that was considered a lot of money).

Jim Hough approached Lansing Schools Superintendent Carl Candoli, convincing him to waive the policy of prohibiting sales on school property in order to allow kids to sell the buttons for fifty cents each. Together, the kids demonstrated their fundraising mettle and sold buttons with astounding enthusiasm. They did so for the privilege of naming the new elephant. Bingham Street School won the contest, selling $720 in buttons, and so the elephant was named in the school's honor: Bingo.

FUZZ THE TORTOISE

Bingo, of course, arrived at the zoo with considerable ceremony and press coverage. However grand her addition to the zoo might have been, it was no match for the even more peculiar ceremony that would follow later that same year. Jim Hough, on one of his many solicitation trips, decided to approach Capital Lodge 141 of the Fraternal Order of Police for the next donation. He told them that the Friends wanted to buy a giant land tortoise at a cost of $1,000. The lodge readily agreed to the proposal, but they were also trying to help fund other community donations, so they presented the zoo with $500. Another $300 came from Frederick Davids, a former director for the state police and at the time public safety director for the University of Michigan; the Friends chipped in the last $200 that was needed. Because of the source of the majority of the donations, the new tortoise would be named "Fuzz," which was a slang term for the police at the time. A more popular—and derogatory—term in those years was "Pig," but though the police were good-humored about the donation, calling a turtle a swine just did not quite fit.

"Everybody in the whole countryside was there,"[1] Hough recalled of the day when Fuzz came to Potter Park. The police gave the tortoise an official escort, with patrol cars sounding their sirens and flashing their lights. Instead of bringing Fuzz into the zoo proper, they dropped him off on Pennsylvania Avenue, just outside the entrance to the park.

Not all the police were informed of what was going on, however. Two patrolmen, Pete Leopke and Butch Bannon, were near the zoo at the time and received an unlikely call from the dispatcher to escort a giant tortoise to Potter Park. At first thinking it was a joke, the two men were eventually convinced this was the real deal. With one on a motorcycle and the other in a patrol car, they indeed found a turtle outside the zoo and proceeded to follow him in.

(Left to right) Zoo staff Bill Swix, Bruce Snyder, John Luks, and Mary Gandy haul Fuzz the Tortoise from his winter quarters to his summertime exhibit (photo courtesy Potter Park Zoo).

As one might imagine, this was a painfully slow parade. Fuzz would stop, take a few steps, turn in the wrong direction and have to be guided down the right path. Eventually, he entered the gates, much to the excitement of the crowds of children who watched the entire show and who then gathered around the display the zoo had created.

Turtle or Tortoise?

Just why are some reptiles with shells called "turtles" and others are "tortoises"? Belonging to the order Chelonia, turtles and tortoises have been around for about 225 million years. They both have hard outer shells, which are formed from the bone of the hips and shoulders and are covered with a layer of keratin; and they are all cold-blooded reptiles. Turtles, however, spend much of their time in water, and have thus developed such adaptations as webbed toes and a more streamlined shell; tortoises are primarily land dwellers, with more domed shells, no webbing, and they tend to be heavier and slower moving. Tortoises also tend to be herbivores (plant eaters), since plants are easier to "catch" if one is slow and plodding, while turtles are more often carnivores. You can find turtles and tortoises in almost any kind of habitat, from swamps to deserts to oceans. Michigan has 10 native species of turtle, including the painted turtle, eastern box turtle, spotted turtle, and wood turtle, among others.

Fuzz had had a very long journey. He was an Aldabra tortoise from the island of that name located in the Indian Ocean off the coast of Africa. When he arrived in 1972, after being flown in and then trucked across the country, he was twenty-five years old and weighed 200 pounds. Fuzz would remain at Potter Park Zoo into the early 2000s. Visitors could easily pick him out because the zoo keepers had attached a thermometer to the top of his shell to help them monitor his temperature and make sure he did not get too hot or too cold. It was a rather peculiar sight. Aldabra tortoises can live to be over 130 years old, and even though he had many more years of life in him, the zoo decided that, after about thirty years of growing larger and larger, he was getting so big it was best to move him to another zoo. He might not have been the most dynamic animal to ever live at Potter Park Zoo, but Fuzz certainly wins marks for arriving in style.

A Child Friendly Zoo

While interesting new animals were arriving at Potter Park Zoo, new construction was also underway in 1973. The barnyard area was greatly improved, including a new barn building that was made possible through financial contributions from Karl Story, and another new area was created just for children, too. A large enclosed "Free Roaming" area was created in the space that today is now the bongo exhibit. With the help of a $20,000 donation from the *Lansing State Journal* to create the enclosure, the zoo's young visitors could see and pet rabbits, oink at the pigs, bottle feed a goat, get close to a lamb or deer, and see one of the zoo favorites, Charlie the Crow. Charlie was once someone's pet, but the owner had turned him over to the zoo. He was not the only crow there, but he was the most memorable. A highly intelligent bird, as crows tend to be, Charlie was especially adept at mimicry, but his most peculiar talent was imitating himself. Zoo visitors, seeing Charlie, would make what they thought was a crow sound: "Caw! Caw!" Of course, crows don't really sound like that, but Charlie picked up on people's poor attempt to talk to him. Before long, he was saying "Caw! Caw!" just like a human imitating a crow.

The playful Charlie was a humble crow, but still a popular animal at the zoo! (photo courtesy Potter Park Zoo).

Also popular were the kids (not the human kind, but young goats), which were donated each spring by area farmers, who then took them back to their farms in the fall. Sometimes the zoo would put the call out in the local newspapers for farmers to donate some of their kids (though usually the same farmers donated animals each year), and those who agreed would have their baby goats taken care of by the zoo over the summer. The society sold bottles of formula to the children for twenty-five cents apiece, a plan that raised as much as $9,000 in 1973. Later, however, it was discovered that bottle feeding the kids sometimes led to "sore mouth," a condition caused by a virus that humans can also contract. Bottle feeding was therefore discontinued in 1987.

Money donations and other forms of volunteered aid were flowing into Potter Park Zoo in the early 1970s for the Free Roaming area and other projects. According to one *Lansing State Journal* article by Jim Hough,[2] some of the zoo's generous contributors included Oldsmobile dealer Karl Story, who gave $7,000 towards the children's zoo, the YMCA Indian Guides, who donated $1,200 for the construction of an overlook for Monkey Island, new exhibit construction to house rheas, a tapir, and the bison that was funded with an $8,000 gift from

Back in the 1970s and '80s, the Barnyard at the zoo featured lots of room and interesting things to climb on for the kids (photo by Susan Owens).

The original pony ride at the zoo featured ponies on a fixed carousel. Today, the rides allow the ponies to walk more freely on an open path (photo by Susan Owens).

Michigan National Bank, $6,000 from the Lansing Sport and Marine Dealers Association to build an outdoor classroom, and $4,000 from the Lansing Jaycees for the waterfowl and duck pond exhibit. Schools in the nearby city of Holt also raised money to help the zoo purchase river otters.

Not all the donations were monetary, however. Construction supplies and services were also contributed. For example, when the parking lot area was being built for the children's zoo, trucks to haul gravel were donated by W.D. White Co. and Brown Brothers Construction, and Teamsters Local 580 provided drivers free of charge.

A unique and unusual gift was presented to Potter Park in 1975 that has now become one of the zoo's most recognized fixtures. In August 1975, Hungarian sculptor Peter Toth began construction of the Indian sculpture near the zoo's entrance. Using an elm tree for his material, he spent nearly two months creating a totem-pole-like work

The Indian Totem wooden sculpture by Peter Toth has become a Potter Park Zoo landmark (photo by Kevin Hile).

of art known as the "Indian Statue." Weighing 7.5 tons and standing over thirty feet high, it is an impressive wooden tribute to Native Americans and one of many such works that Toth planned to construct throughout the United States. Money for the statue was donated by the Lansing Indian Center. After completing his work, Toth, a rather mysterious figure, disappeared and did not make contact again with the zoo for nearly three decades. Recently, zoo officials began to fret as the Indian Statue showed its age and a crack began to develop in it that threatened to compromise its structure. Then, in 2005, Toth just as mysteriously reappeared without previous announcement of his intentions, as if out of nowhere. He repaired the statue free of charge as his gift to Potter Park, then departed without another word.

Such donations as these were not always tallied up in terms of dollars, but it was estimated that over $250,000 in goods and services had been donated between the founding of the Friends of the Zoo in 1969 and 1975.

Not surprisingly, such energy and community involvement helped boost zoo attendance, and by 1975 Potter Park was seeing over 400,000 guests passing through its gates annually. "Our attendance has more than doubled since 1969, when the Zoo Society was formed," director Gerry Miller reported in 1976.[3]

A SHORT HISTORY OF THE ZOO TRAIN

Another draw to the zoo came in the summer of 1974, when Haslett resident Dave Aldrich proposed the installation of a train ride on zoo grounds. Building the track himself and with the aid of Joe Christophel, Aldrich constructed a route that began at a rustic train station just behind where the totem pole is located today. It then wended its way near the old gift shop and the former zoo entrance. Traveling east, the train entered a short tunnel (also built by Aldrich), chugged and chuffed its way toward the area that would become the aviary by the Patagonian hare exhibit (also known as a Patagonian cavy or mara), and then turned back westward. The diminutive locomotive then passed by the sika (Alaskan) and white-tailed deer exhibit before ending up back at the station.

The charge for the delightful trip through the woods by rail was initially thirty-five cents per customer. Soon, the Friends of the Zoo created a package that included the train ride, a pony ride, hot dog and chips, all for $1.65. Aldrich would get some of this money, and the zoo kept the rest.

The zoo's train ride was a big hit with children (photos courtesy Susan Owens).

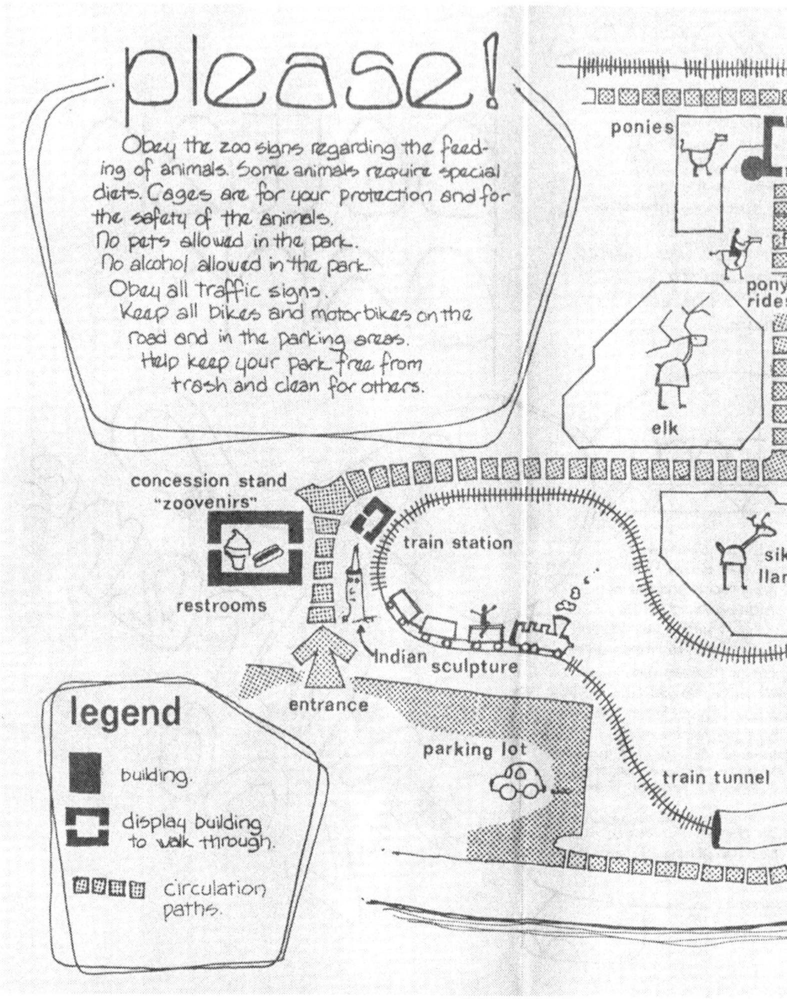

This old undated map shows the route of the zoo train (photo courtesy Potter Park

This partnership continued successfully until 1986. The death knell for the train ride was rung by skyrocketing liability insurance rates. When Aldrich first began his operation, his insurance payments ate up eight percent of his income; by 1986 this had jumped to 24.8 percent. Aldrich complained that the City of Lansing's insistence that he carry a $1,000,000 policy, plus its unwillingness to shop for a cheaper policy, forced his hand. City Attorney Stephen Sawyer and Doug Finley, who was then director of the Parks and Recreation Department, argued that the train concessionaire should

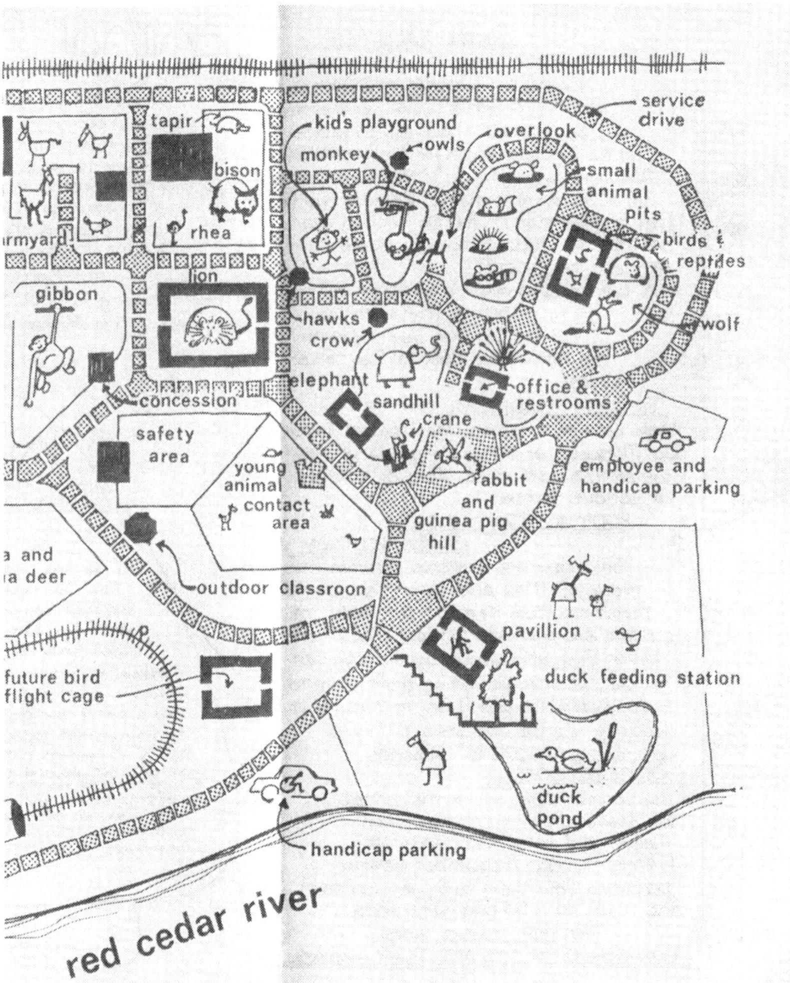

Zoo Society).

carry the same amount of insurance as John Chamberlain, who ran the Red Cedar river boat ride. At an impasse, Aldrich disassembled the tracks, loaded up the engine and railroad cars, and looked elsewhere for his business operation. The train station was converted into a gift shop, which was later razed. Today, all that remains to remind us the zoo once had a train is the tunnel Aldrich built, which is now used each Halloween as the "Boo Tunnel," where volunteers dress up in costumes and spook brave children who dare to enter the darkened corridor.

When the train operation closed, the zoo still planned to build a train ride that would become part of the new experience of a revitalized zoo. This proposal, however, would never come to fruition.

FLOOD, FOLLOWED BY A GOOD CHANCE OF FRISKY FELINES

One of the most memorable events at Potter Park during the 1970s came in 1975, when one of the worst floods ever experienced in Lansing struck the zoo. Nestled next to the Red Cedar River, the zoo and park benefit from a bucolic piece of real estate that is home to large populations of Canada geese, Mallard ducks, swans, and other waterfowl. Every spring, like clockwork, the waters will spill over the banks and typically encroach onto the parking lot. In 1975, however, the water level rose and rose and rose and ROSE! It became so deep that it covered the chain link fence around the zoo; Bill Swix recalled how one motorboat pilot steered his craft so close to the zoo that he actually was able to navigate his vessel over the fence.

As retired zoo keeper Bruce Snyder remembered, no animals were in serious danger during the flood. The staff had to move some of the animals that were kept near the duck pond, sandbags were placed around the Bird House (mostly to protect the office that was in the

The old entrance to the zoo is partially underwater during the 1975 flood (photo courtesy Potter Park Zoo).

building's basement), and there was considerable flooding near Monkey Island, though the stone wall around the enclosure easily protected the spider monkeys and aoudads. Fortunately, most of the zoo grounds are situated on a low hill, placing the majority of exhibits out of harm's way. Still, the zoo had to be closed to visitors for about a week, since no one could enter the parking lot.

A more joyful cause for excitement came in November 1976, when Potter Park Zoo greeted the birth of two African lion cubs. At the time, the lioness Juliet II had only been at the zoo for three weeks (and had not even been introduced to her new mate, Romeo). She was the replacement for the first Juliet, who had died a few months earlier. Unbeknownst to anyone, she was already pregnant when she arrived at Potter Park from another zoo, and nobody knew she was about to give birth. Juliet II had three cubs and was an excellent mother, but when one of the cubs died of pneumonia, the staff decided to hand raise the other two, just to be safe.

The cubs were soon given names: Butch and Sunnie. It was the most exciting event to happen at the zoo since Bingo arrived. The successful birth of African lions at such a small zoo was a rare event, and their youthful antics and speedy growth soon made them a handful.

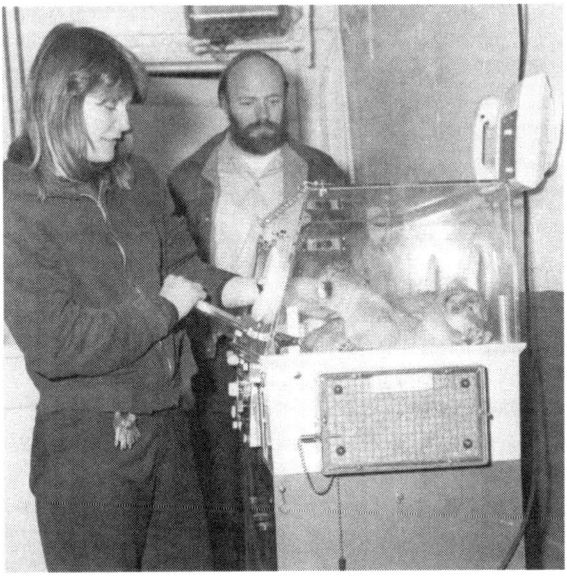

Keepers Jan Brigham and Dave Dickert watch over the little lion cubs Butch and Sunnie (photo courtesy Potter Park Zoo).

After just five months, they had grown to about fifty pounds each and were becoming too much for the keepers to handle. Still, the staff often let Butch and Sunnie explore places probably better left to house cats. In one incident, for example, some of the keepers decided to play a joke on Bill Swix. He was eating lunch in his office, when the door opened and in walked the two cubs, who had been let in by the jokesters. They leapt onto his desk, skidding across the papers and turning Swix's office into a shambles. In another frolicsome incident, one of the cubs bit maintenance supervisor Ron Moore on the buttocks while he was speaking to Swix over the intercom. The conversation was interrupted by a startled yelp from Moore.

Zoos in the 1970s

While the Friends of the Zoo were doing much to rejuvenate Potter Park Zoo in the 1970s, other zoos around the country were leading the way in exhibit design. Building on the earlier work of Heine Hediger, landscape architects Grant Jones and Jon Coe developed the concept of "landscape immersion." Beginning with the Woodland Park Zoo in Seattle, Washington, they built a groundbreaking gorilla exhibit that not only followed Hediger's concepts on creating a natural environment, but also created the impression for visitors that they were actually *inside* the enclosure with the gorillas. This was done by extending the environment outside the actual exhibit so that zoo guests would find themselves among plants and, in the case of this particular exhibit, birds from the African jungles. Such designs would become increasingly common in larger zoos in the United States, while smaller zoos like Potter Park focused on simply providing better animal care and more educational experiences for visitors.

CHIMPS AND GIBBONS AND BEARS, OH MY!

Other popular animals at Potter Park Zoo during the 1970s included chimpanzees, gibbons, black bears, tigers, otters, and, of course, Bingo the elephant. Suzie the lion was one of Bill Swix's favorite animals. "She was a good gal," he recalled fondly. Her personality came out in such incidents as when zoo keeper Lisle Skutt decided one day to check the lion's teeth. Skutt, Swix related, "lifted her lip up to see how the teeth looked," but Suzie decided she wanted none of that. She held on to one of the keeper's fingers. Skutt had to put his fingers up her nose "so she couldn't breathe, so she opened her mouth up and he got his finger back."[4] Suzie didn't damage the finger, however. She could be stubborn, but gentle. Potter Park had a succession of tigers over the years, including Bo and Tony the Tiger (who were half-brothers), the latter named after the famous cereal box character, and many others. The most famous was probably Ivan, who was one of the longest-lived tigers in American zoo history when he passed away in 2003 at the age of twenty.

The zoo had several chimps over the years, sometimes having two together, and sometimes just a lone chimp. During the mid-1960s, Adam the chimp was a favorite resident at the zoo. "Adam was kind of neat," said Swix. "He was a chimp we got from the Brookfield Zoo in Chicago, when Marlin Perkins [the former television host of *Mutual of Omaha's Wild Kingdom*] was there. He'd been taken away from some farmer who had trained Adam to drive his tractor and everything else on the farm, as I understand. Adam was a big guy, and tough! He used to take a golf ball and take it all apart with his teeth. He took all the little rubber bands inside and had them stretched out all over. He made a heck of a mess! We would clean his cage up, and the next day it seemed there was just that much left. He'd hide it all somewhere." After Adam passed away in 1966, Nancy and Zippy were brought to the zoo from Liberia and were there until the 1970s, the last few years of which Nancy was by herself after Zippy died.

For a short time during the 1970s, the zoo also kept mountain lions named Skeeter and Sulie. In 1979, when Michigan State University's men's basketball team won the national title, Sulie gave birth to twin female cubs. The cubs were named Magic, in honor of Earvin "Magic" Johnson, and Special K, after the nickname of another Spartan star, Gregory Kelser.

Popular primates at the zoo included the spider monkeys, gibbons, and hamadrayas baboons. Before the outdoor enclosure was built for the monkeys in 1987, the spider monkeys were kept on Monkey Island, along with the aoudads. This made for a rather unusual exhibit by modern zoo standards. The current philosophy is to have animals from the same continent living together, but spider monkeys are from South America, while aoudads are from Africa. "What was interesting," recalled Sonny Lumbert, "was that if the monkeys started harassing the [aoudads], they would just climb to the highest rock."[5] In one case, however, a spider monkey kept trying to bite the aoudads. This resulted in the keepers finally deciding to remove the monkey's canine teeth.

Keepers Dave Dickert and Jan Brigham hold the cubs Magic and Special K (photo courtesy Potter Park Zoo).

The tooth extraction occurred sometime before Dr. Jim Sikarskie, a vet from MSU who was long associated with Potter Park Zoo, began working for the zoo in 1975, and he emphasized to me recently that such medically unnecessary dental work would not have been approved by him. These days, rather than pulling his teeth, the spider monkey would have been moved somewhere else.

Potter Park Zoo had good luck with its baboons, with four babies being born in 1979. And the white-handed gibbons proved feisty and popular attractions. The gibbons were the species that was originally in the outdoor exhibit where the spider monkeys are currently quartered. According to keeper Jan Brigham (daughter-in-law of Fenner Nature Center naturalist Joan Brigham), the outside exhibit was built in order to give the gibbons some fresh air because they had been kept strictly inside the Feline/Primate House. The outdoor structure, constructed with funding that included $3,000 from the Lansing Junior League and the *Lansing State Journal,* included an outside area surrounded by fencing, plus a small wooden building that was heated. Unfortunately, the gibbons were not smart enough to know that they should go inside that building during cold weather. On one night, when there was a freezing rain, the female gibbon did not go inside.

The next day, the keepers found that she had frostbite so severe she had to be euthanized. Soon after that, in 1987, a larger, more inviting indoor quarters was built with financing from the Friends of the Zoo.

A visitor to Potter Park Zoo in the 1970s could also enjoy seeing such sights as Brazilian tapirs, Grant's zebras in the barnyard area, and Australian dingoes and African Cape hunting dogs in the Dog House area. Also popular were the zoo's two black bears, Yogi and Boo Boo. Originally, the bear exhibit had been adjacent to the Dog House, but several "large moat" areas were later built in 1958 behind the Bird/Reptile House (on the east side of the building). The four exhibits here, which have since been closed, also housed crab-eating fox, wolves, and coyotes on various occasions.

Yogi and Boo Boo were favorites for many years at Potter Park. Though both black bears, Yogi, the male, was a cinnamon color, while Boo Boo, the female, was indeed black. Actually, the Boo Boo that most guests remember was the second bear to have that name. The original Boo Boo had died unexpectedly at a young age. These black bears were among keeper Mary Anne McNamara's favorites. One of the highlights of her daily duties was cleaning out the bear exhibit. The large moats were aligned side by side, with large partitions between each made of concrete. In front of the exhibits was a drainage area, and in front of that a wall to separate zoo visitors from the animals. The animals then had an outside area and an inside holding area out of the public's view that was accessible through a door in the back of the exhibit. The only way to clean out the exhibits efficiently, then, was for the keepers to stand atop the rear wall that overlooked them and spray down onto the concrete below with a hose. On the roof, behind the rear wall, was a pulley system that operated the divider doors between the inside holding areas, as well as the doors to the outside exhibit areas. After flushing these exhibits, the water and waste would flow into a lower moat that would then drain into a sump where it would be pumped out into the sewers. Valves had to be operated to drain the dirty water out.

It was a fairly elaborate system, but the keepers soon noticed that the bears were fascinated by the stream of water that sprayed down on them each day. "One day," McNamara remembered, "Yogi climbed into the pool and sat down to enjoy the water from the big fire hoses that we used to use. They had an incredible amount of force and pressure. We kind of started gently hosing the side of the pool or the floor of the yard right next to the pool so that he would get the splash over, but not the full force of the hose. He apparently really enjoyed that!

So it became a routine. When the weather was warm, usually April to September or October, every day when we got to clean the bear moat, if Yogi chose to get into the pool, we would then hose him. We would hose him for quite a while! Although we were doing our job, sometimes it was almost as much of a break for us as it was for him.

"After a while, we would actually start spraying the water on him, or in the pool in front of him, and we'd move the hose around so we didn't spray him too directly on one spot constantly. Yogi would turn around for you to spray his back, and when he felt he was done he would turn around again so you could do his stomach. And he'd lean back and stick his feet up so you could do his feet."[6]

The sight of Yogi getting a shower from the keepers always drew attention from the public, as well as media coverage on occasion.

By far the most popular of the animals at Potter Park Zoo during the 1970s, however, was Bingo. Her story, and the story of her successor, Tombi, would become one of the most important chapters in Potter Park Zoo's history.

4

Once There Were Elephants: The Story of Bingo and Tombi

When people visit a zoo, there are certain species that they always expect to see. Among these are usually the African and Asian animals that come to mind when we think of wildlife, including giraffes, zebras, lions, gorillas, chimpanzees, hippopotami, tigers, pandas, and rhinoceroses. Such animals comprise what are sometimes referred to by wildlife professionals as "charismatic megavertebrates." One of the most impressive of these is the elephant.

The Remarkable Asian Elephant

Elephants are remarkable mammals whose numbers are declining precipitously, especially in Asia. Around the year 1900, there were about 100,000 elephants in Thailand, the land formerly known as Siam that Bingo called her birthplace. Today, that number is down to about 3,500, largely because of habitat loss and poaching. It is a shame that such a fate has come to pass for these remarkable creatures that resemble people in so many ways. Having a life span of about 60 years, elephants are social animals who spend the first sixteen or so years of their lives—about the time females are ready to bear their first young—learning from their elders. They are amazingly intelligent and curious creatures, and enjoy rich, complex family lives. Of course, their anatomy is very different from ours. Bulls (male elephants) can weigh up to 12,000 pounds, while cows (females) can be as much as 10,000 pounds. Their hearing is extraordinary, and scientists now know they can detect subsonic sounds and even ground vibrations from miles away through their feet. Also, there's that amazing trunk, which has 100,000 individual muscles, making this useful limb (actually an evolved upper lip) so strong it can pick up a log with ease, yet so versatile it can also grab a leaf, peanut, or toothpick with its prehensile tip.

Purchased through the fund raising efforts of the Friends of the Zoo, Bingo was born in Phetchabun, which is about a hundred miles north of Bangkok, in June 1972. Her price tag was $3,500, and it cost almost that much to ship the five-month-old pachyderm in a specially pressurized airplane cabin. Various details and difficulties with arrangements meant that Bingo did not arrive at the zoo until November 1972, when it was already becoming quite cold in Michigan for a tropical animal.

Baby Bingo was an instant hit with kids, who were often allowed to visit the little elephant up close (photo courtesy Potter Park Zoo).

To keep Bingo warm and safe, she was quarantined indoors all winter. Weighing less than 200 pounds at the time, she was fed a diet consisting of Gerber Baby Food, Pet milk, baby oatmeal, water, and vitamin and iron supplements.

Bingo's arrival was a media event. In an article in the *Lansing State Journal,* Jim Hough reported on the press conference. Students from Bingham Street School were invited to attend, and zoo supervisor Jerry Miller introduced the baby elephant to everyone. As Hough observed, Miller was "acting like a proud father."[1] In fact, he had doled out cigars to the zoo staff, and on each one was written "It's a Girl!"

For shelter, the zoo staff had to improvise for Bingo, and the elephant was kept in the basement of the Bird House so she would be warm and safe during the cold winter months. This made for difficult public viewing, however, and only a few visitors at a time were allowed inside to see Bingo during limited late-morning and early afternoon hours. Those who got to see her instantly fell in love with the sweet elephant baby, who rubbed her trunk delicately on guest's faces and cried when they left her alone.

HOUSING PROBLEMS

One thing that all baby animals have in common is that they grow up. While for some creatures, such as monkeys, this is not a particular problem at a zoo, with an elephant it is a very different matter. Female Asian elephants can grow to be between eight and nine feet tall and weigh between 8,000 and 10,000 pounds when fully grown, which is in their twenties. Since elephants can live to be about sixty years old, finding space for Bingo was not going to be a temporary challenge. The zoo would need a sizeable exhibit for Bingo without delay.

As a juvenile, Bingo's rate of growth was remarkable. She added about 1.5 feet in height and hundreds of pounds each year, topping 1,200 pounds by 1975; by the next year, she was almost 3,000 pounds and six feet tall, plus her tusks were beginning to emerge. During the winter, this was especially a problem. Bingo's quarters in the Bird House basement were not very large, and at night, after the keepers had left, the curious little elephant discovered that she was able to reach lots of interesting things with her long trunk, including water pipes and ceiling light fixtures. "In fact, one time," recalled keeper Bruce Snyder, "I think it was either Christmas Eve or New Year's

Eve, we noticed the next morning that she had gotten the lock off the door and destroyed everything in the bottom of the Bird House. They used to have a big pile of sand that they used to use for the bird cages. She played in that; she broke rakes. But when we looked in on her in the morning, she was back in her exhibit waiting for her bottle."[2] By January of 1974 Miller was beginning to fret that if they did not do something quickly, the zoo would have to give Bingo up, possibly to a circus. The idea was then to get another infant elephant, but the flaw of that logic was readily apparent: a new baby elephant would grow quickly, too, and then the zoo would be back to square one.

In a case of déja vu reflecting back to 1969, when the Friends were founded because of concerns with the zoo's decline, Potter Park once again found itself under the scrutiny of a federal veterinarian, who quickly pointed out the inadequacy of Bingo's winter home. This was in addition to a renewed complaint over the state of the Feline/Primate House, which still suffered from poor ventilation. Working up an estimate for a new elephant exhibit, the zoo predicted it would cost between $20,000 and $30,000 for an elephant house.

The new elephant house was built for Bingo with money raised by the Friends of the Zoo (photo courtesy Potter Park Zoo).

The Friends of the Zoo sprang into action and began raising money, and by October of 1974 they had put a $7,000 dent in the fund for the exhibit. The public also offered proposals for Bingo fund raisers. As Mike Hughes wrote in a *Lansing State Journal* article, "One involves asking a restaurant chain to hold a promotional gimmick for Bingo. Another involves asking local bingo parlors to hold a special 'bingo for Bingo' night."[3]

The most helpful proposal, however, came from Associated Builders and Contractors (ABC), Central Michigan Chapter, which generously offered to donate materials and labor costs for a new Bingo shelter to the city. It did not take the Lansing City Council long to accept their largesse. However, there were other matters that needed to be attended to. Even with a new winter shelter building, Bingo did not have an adequate outdoor exhibit. Initially, the elephant exhibit was located near the dog house, and was little more than a wooden building and a chain to keep Bingo from leaving the area. What she really needed was a walled off moat enclosure that would allow her to walk about outside freely.

The City Council refused to pay for an additional $29,000 for the outdoor elephant moat, and so it once more fell to the Friends and private organizations to help. Yet again, it was ABC to the rescue; they donated materials and labor so that when the entire elephant exhibit was completed in 1975, they had effectively given the zoo $60,000. Jim Hough gave ABC due credit in his "The Onlooker" column in July 1975: "Associated Builders & Contractors ... made a full commitment to the project. And they didn't skimp. It's a great job." Hough added, "It's a tremendous addition to the zoo.... They bailed Bingo and the children of Lansing out of a predicament."[4] The generosity of ABC's contribution was matched only by the City Council's parsimony.

Boisterous Bingo

Everyone loved Bingo at Potter Park Zoo: visitors, keepers, staff, and the press. Like Herman the Mexican burro before her, she became the star and main attraction. To those who remember her, Bingo was no ordinary little Asian elephant. She had a definite playful, spunky attitude that endeared her to one and all. Being an only child, so to speak, she was very much a pampered animal as well. Each morning, before the gates opened to allow the day's guests inside, the keepers would take Bingo out for a walk around the grounds to stretch her legs. Walking is extremely important to elephants, who need such exercise to keep their feet healthy. Another part of the morning routine was her oil rubdown. Keepers Bruce Snyder and Morrice "Bub" Dunn would rub Bingo all over with about two quarts of vegetable oil to keep her skin from becoming too dry, which was especially vital during Michigan's winters.

Bingo also received regular haircuts and pedicures, and her keepers would occupy her curious mind by teaching her tricks. Elephants are known to be one of the most intelligent species on the planet, and so if they are not regularly stimulated with activities, they become easily bored. And a bored elephant can be a destructive, dangerous creature.

Bingo was most definitely not a trained circus elephant, and she was not used as an elephant ride attraction to raise money for the zoo. Nevertheless, sometimes the keepers would permit certain people to ride her. One special case involved children from the Michigan School for the Blind, who were invited to ride her quite often. The staff would allow the sight-impaired kids to rub their hands all over Bingo and then try to draw pictures of her. The keepers sometimes gave themselves a treat and rode her briefly, too, or they would allow their relatives to do so; and on Clown Days a clown might be seen on her back for a special promotional photograph (see page 40).

(From left to right) Dave Dickert, along with his wife, Jo, and son Todd (behind Bingo) give Bingo some fun outside time with keeper Bub Dunn (photo courtesy Potter Park Zoo).

Bruce Snyder was one of the keepers who was in charge of Bingo's care, along with Bub Dunn. "She was definitely a crowd favorite," he reflected. In fact, Snyder confessed, "that was the reason I became a zoo keeper, because I knew I was going to get to work with the elephant." Bingo was a handful, though, and often quite naughty. In the summer, before ABC had built the larger elephant house but after she had been forced to stay in the Bird House basement, she was kept in a smaller wooden building. Here she broke the lock to the door and once damaged a water pipe. Bingo mixed the water with the surrounding dirt to create her own makeshift mud bath—an elephant's private spa! Once in her new exhibit, however, her behavior was no less mischievous. When staff at the zoo tried to make the area around Bingo's enclosure more pleasant by planting sod around it, the young pachyderm had a raucous time tearing it all out with her trunk and throwing it onto her back—another habit of elephants, who like to use dirt to protect their skin from the sun and parasites.

Perhaps it was because of Bingo's outgoing personality and charm that people started to take special interest in her treatment at the zoo. In the winter, when guests were few, Bingo seemed lonely from the perspective of visitors. Because of space limitations at the zoo, Potter Park never had more than one elephant. At the time, as Bruce Snyder later admitted, keepers did not worry about this too much, because they were not fully aware of the importance of family groups—herds—to elephants and how much they can suffer when alone. Another concern was the chain around Bingo's ankle. There were a number of legitimate reasons for Bingo's leg chain, but many zoo guests did not understand. To them, it seemed a cruel practice.

"I'm not going to that zoo till they get that chain off her leg," a little girl reportedly complained in a *Lansing State Journal* article by Dan Poorman. The unnamed girl also said, "It looked so sad when I went there, she tried to come to me but couldn't, it (the chain) yanked her leg."[5]

The staff and volunteers at Potter Park Zoo, however, understood just why the chain was necessary. It was needed to keep Bingo from damaging her quarters, to maintain control of the elephant when the keepers were handling her or when Bingo was being petted by a zoo guest, and to keep the animal docile around humans. Furthermore, it was no more painful to Bingo than a collar is around a dog's neck. Many staff hours were spent getting Bingo acclimated to the chain, and she only wore it an average of five hours a day. Without such constraints, it was a definite possibility that Bingo would become more aggressive and dominant, and a 3,000-pound pachyderm could easily throw a man across a room with its trunk or charge through a chain link or wooden fence.

BINGO LEAVES THE ZOO, ALL TOO SOON

Indeed, a huge Asian elephant could be a danger to visitors and staff, but it turned out in the end that Bingo was a danger to herself. This would result in one of the most tragic chapters in Potter Park Zoo's history.

In 1979, Bingo's keepers noticed that she was behaving oddly and seemed to be having trouble eating. Calling Dr. Jim Sikarskie, the on-call vet at Michigan State University's College of Veterinary Medicine, the staff learned that the young elephant had swallowed a stone about the size of a baseball. How this happened, no one was certain, though Bingo had developed a habit of picking up things she found and putting them in her mouth. In the past, she had swallowed such objects as a baseball cap, a lock, and even a mitten. Bruce Snyder noted that she had swallowed fairly large inedible objects before with no problems, but this time, the rock lodged in Bingo's throat.

There was no other course of action but surgery. Dr. Sikarskie—still a young vet who had graduated just a few years earlier—called a board-certified equine surgeon, Dr. John Stick, as well as a certified anesthesiologist. Working together with the help of Bruce Snyder, Nancy Harger, and Earl Austin to help handle and calm Bingo, the anesthesia was administered by the vets. The medical team then set to work on the groundbreaking surgery. Using a fiberoptic scope in a procedure that, for 1979, was cutting edge, the surgeon looked down Bingo's esophagus to locate the stone and assess the damage. Because general anesthesia would have put the elephant's life at risk, only local anesthesia was used while Bingo remained standing and under the constant watch and care of her keepers.

After removing the rock, the surgeon did not sew up the wound because previous research on horses showed that this would have led to the development of scar tissue that would have made it difficult for Bingo to swallow, even after she had healed. Instead, after she had recovered enough from the operation, the vets fed Bingo using a bilge pump that led into her incision and to her stomach. Periodically, a fiberoptic scope was used to evaluate the slow healing process; restraints and tranquilizers again had to be used while Bingo was under anesthesia.

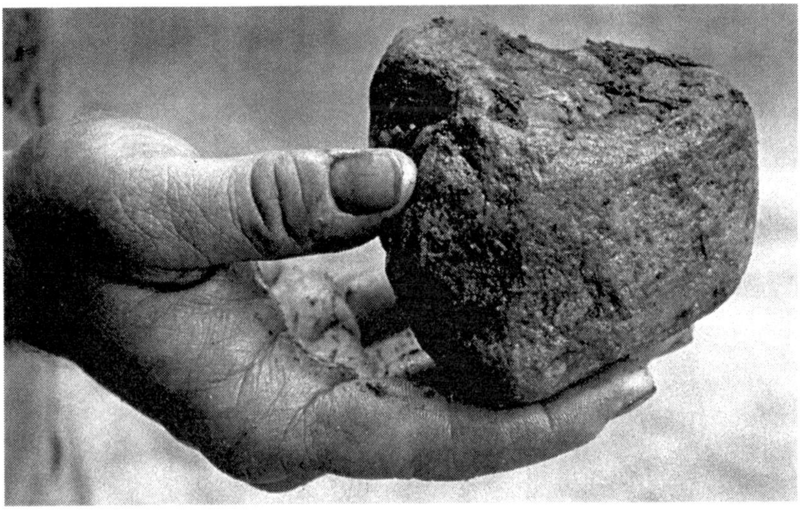

The stone that caused all the trouble (photo by Norris Ingells courtesy Melissa Ingells).

After hours of strenuous, worrisome surgery, the rock was removed. Fed through a tube, Bingo recovered slowly, but the operation was considered a success. The young zoo star was permitted to appear in public again and was the recipient of hundreds of letters from school children wishing her a speedy recovery. By the end of June 1979, she seemed to be doing well, and as a welcome back she was provided with a new sandbox to play in.

Then, unexpectedly, Bingo showed signs of illness again. An examination showed that the elephant had developed a throat infection. No blockage was discovered, but the infection was a serious concern. Dr. Sikarskie explained what happened next:

> What had happened was that she had eaten some [food] pellets, and when the swallowing reflexes returned to the damaged area, some of the pellets would reflux back, and when she breathed them in they entered her lungs. An elephant can sleep standing up, so you can't hear their lungs very well.... On necropsy [an autopsy for animals] we found grain in her lungs ... and she had fungus growing on that grain.[6]

As a result, Bingo developed pneumonia before vets understood what was going on, for they could hear nothing wrong when they listened to her lungs, and when they examined her throat she appeared to be healing just fine. They also could not see that Bingo's liver was

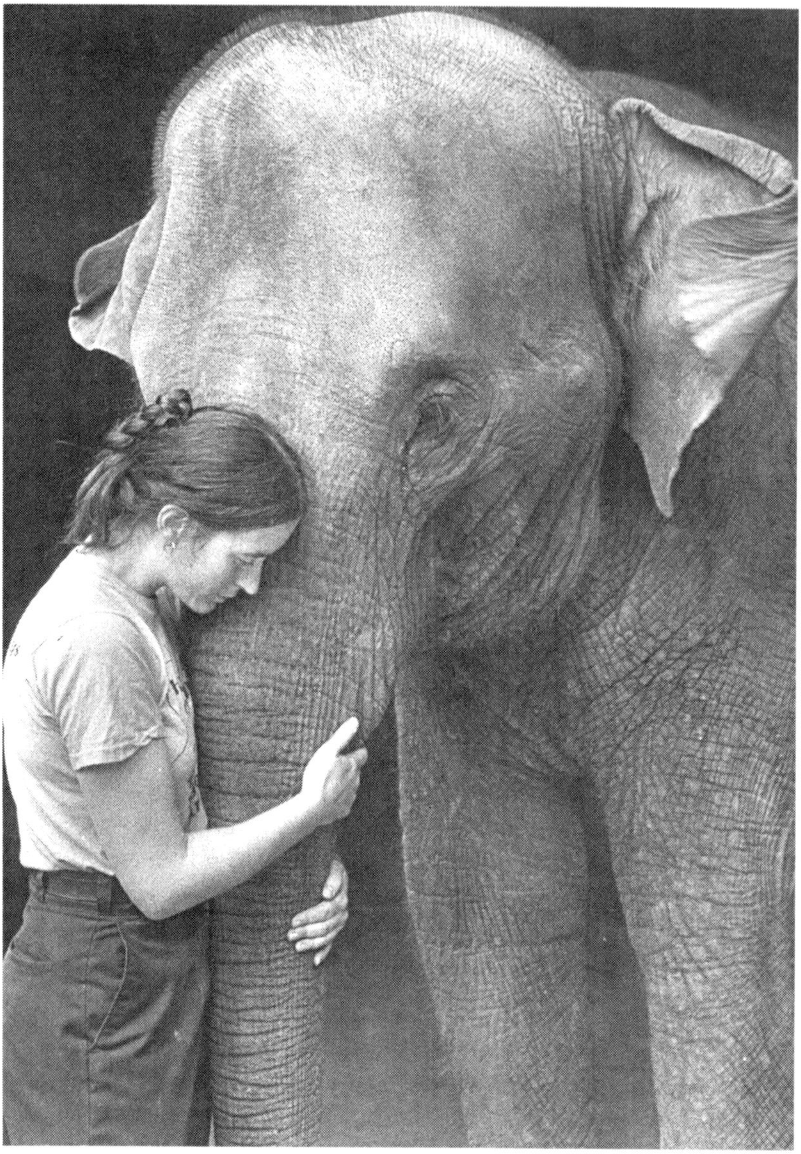

Keeper Nancy Harger comforts Bingo before surgery. Keepers play an essential role in veterinary medicine at the zoo, especially when it comes to calming animal patients (photo by Norris Ingells courtesy Melissa Ingells).

being severely damaged by toxins as a side-effect of the pneumonia. By early August, Bingo seemed to still be recuperating and doing fine. It wasn't until August 13, 1979, that she suddenly refused food,

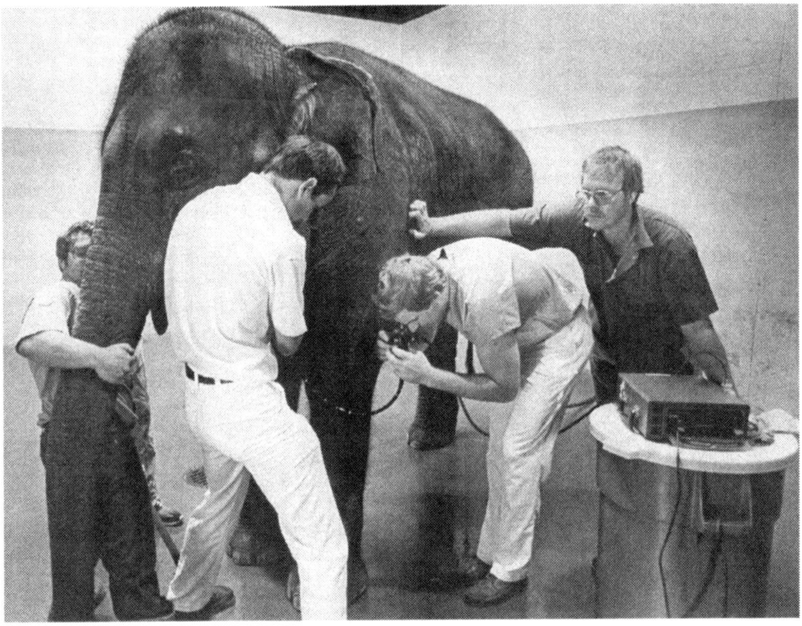

Vets use a fiberoptic scope to examine the blockage in Bingo's throat (photo by Norris Ingells courtesy Melissa Ingells).

and the staff knew then something was wrong. If the elephant did not get her 45 pounds of food and 50 gallons of water a day, she would slowly dehydrate and starve to death.

Then Bingo fell over onto her side. Moments later, she was gone.

She was just seven years old.

Bingo's death left the zoo's staff in complete shock and bewilderment. The next day, *Lansing State Journal* reporter Mark Nixon tried to convey the mood at the zoo: "Long-faced zoo keepers wandered around the silent elephant house today, some barely able to restrain tears."[7]

Since an elephant, even one as beloved and special as Bingo, can't be buried, her remains were cremated. A memorial marker was placed in the zoo dedicated to Bingo as a remembrance, but even that is now gone.

THE ELEPHANT DEBATE

The death of Bingo left zoo staff and the community in shock. Now the question became, should the zoo get another elephant to

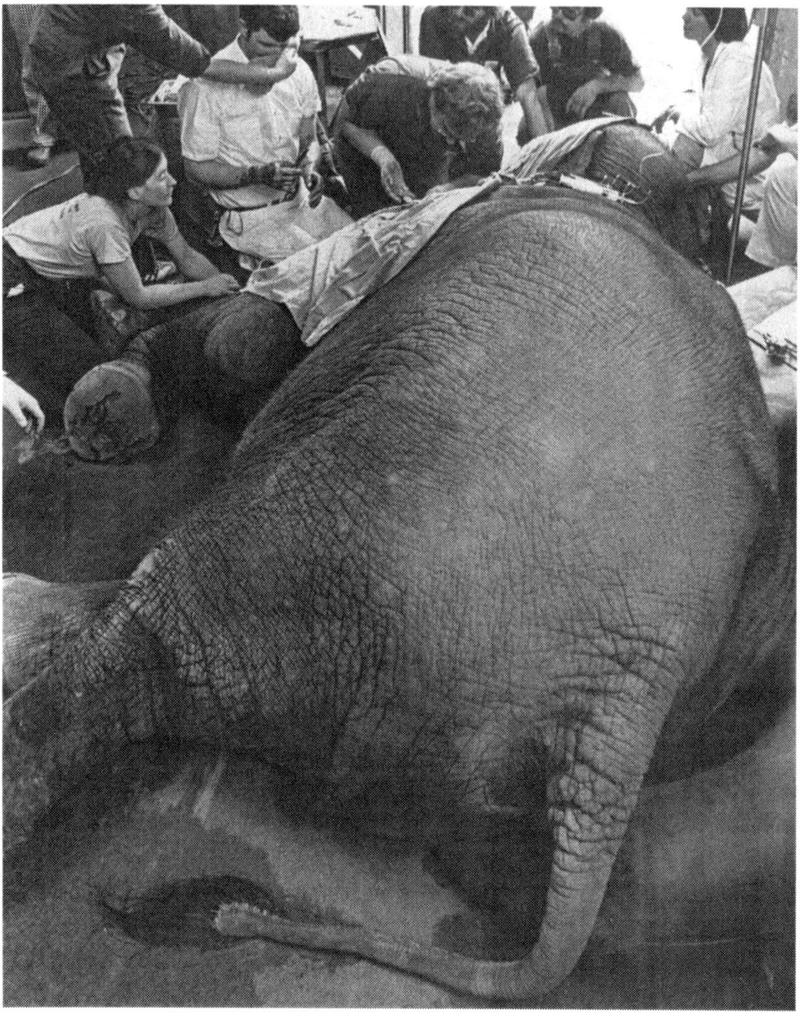

There were so many veterinarians, vet students, keepers, and other zoo staff wanting to help during the surgery that there was almost no room for Bingo! (photo by Norris Ingells courtesy Melissa Ingells).

replace her? When Bingo had come to Potter Park Zoo in 1972, there was overwhelming support for the addition of an elephant at Lansing's zoo. Seven years later, however, a second school of thought had emerged that keeping such large mammals confined to a little zoo with limited resources was cruel. This view was aptly expressed by Lansing resident Amy C. Schumacher, who wrote a letter to the *Lansing State Journal*'s opinion page:

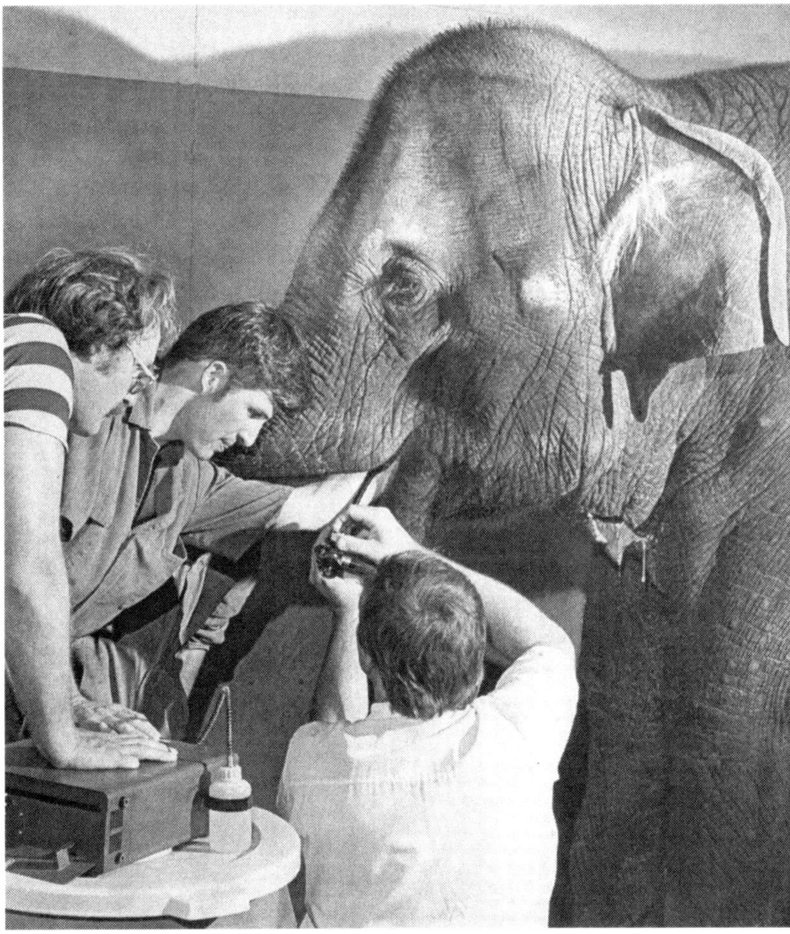

After the surgery, Bingo was fed through a tube in her throat. Dr. Sikarskie (far left) observes as MSU vets check on the elephant's progress (photo by Norris Ingells courtesy Melissa Ingells).

> I cannot believe that this animal did not experience loneliness, sadness, or boredom.... I believe that if the children of this community were made aware of the indignities and unhappiness that Bingo suffered, they would not wish this same condition on another elephant. If the Potter Park Zoo is so determined to have another elephant, I plead that they wait until they can create a better environment in which it can exist.[8]

Not long after this letter was published, zoo keeper Jan Brigham also wrote to the newspaper. In her letter, she warned of the dangers of "anthropomorphism," the tendency of people to sometimes attribute human characteristics to non-human species. She also pointed out that "freedom for wild animals" is no longer an issue in a world where elephants, tigers, and many other species are being crowded out by the encroachment of humans into their territories. No longer was it possible, even back in 1979, for Asian elephants, for example, to roam wherever they wished. They were increasingly restricted to smaller and smaller forests in India. In Africa, the situation was much the same; the elephants there all now exist in wildlife preserves. In essence, there are no truly "wild" places left in Africa. They are all managed by governments in parks with defined boundaries.

One problem many people have is that much of what they know of wildlife comes from television programs and movies. Wildlife specials viewed on television give audiences the impression that these animals are free to go wherever they please. However, that is a false impression. Many Americans have also been influenced since childhood by cartoons, such as those produced by Walt Disney Studios, which depict animals in very human-like ways. Though Bingo was indeed a very loveable animal, Brigham tried to point out that the elephant was not a human being. "In my studies," the zoo keeper wrote in her *Lansing State Journal* letter, "I have not found any research data proving animals, excluding primates, experience these kinds of feelings," such as sadness and loneliness.[9]

Jerry Miller also defended the elephant exhibit as being humane and perfectly suited to a pachyderm. "The fact is," he told Jim Hough in "The Onlooker," "our elephant house is bigger and better than the elephant facilities in Toledo, Grand Rapids, and Detroit. The space per elephant is much less in those zoos. What's more, they don't have the soft dirt areas outside for the elephants. Therefore, they have constant foot problems due to walking on cement all summer."[10]

An excellent illustration of how attitudes about elephants in captivity have evolved comes from Jan Brigham, who recently told me that her feelings on the subject have changed considerably since the days when she worked with Bingo: "Much behavior research has been done since then, and we know that elephants mourn those who have died. I know that I felt that the keepers were Bingo's 'herd,' and that is why [I thought] having a single elephant wasn't as bad as some people made it out to be. I may have been wrong."[11]

Differences between Asian and African Elephants

Other than the fact that one comes from Africa and the other from Asia, there are several marked differences between these species. The most obvious is the ears, which are much larger in the African variety. Africans also tend to be larger, with bulls weighing as much as 14,000 pounds, about a ton more than the largest Asian elephant, and Asians have more of a rounded back compared to their cousins. The heads are very different, too; Asian elephants have two obvious humps on their heads. As for the trunks, Africans have two "fingers," or prehensile tips, versus the Asian elephant's one. Tusks in Africans tend to be larger and both sexes possess tusks, while Asian elephants have smaller tusks (actually, they are elongated molars), with cows often having much smaller tusks or none at all. Count the number of toes on these elephants and you will find that Africans usually have four on the foreleg and three on the back, while Asians have five and four, respectively. These are some of the most obvious differences, though there are other more subtle variances.

TOMBI COMES TO TOWN

So it was that Jerry Miller and the City of Lansing decided to heed the pleas from many in the community who wanted an elephant back at their zoo. A hunt for a suitable animal ensued, and by October 1979 Miller had located one who had been brought to the Dallas, Texas, zoo from her birthplace in Africa. Her purchase price was $12,500. An additional $1,500 for transportation and $1,400 for insurance added to the bill. To foot the cost, the Friends of the Zoo responded by raising most of the money needed to buy the new pachyderm. Much of the cash, over $9,000, was donated by Xerox Corporation, which held a phonothon and also collected money from its employees, as well as dipping into the company's own coffers.

When she arrived on November 8, 1979, the elephant already had a name: Tombi. The name, which is Zulu for "girl," stuck because the young pachyderm had already been trained to respond to commands using that name, and it would have been too difficult to retrain her. A little larger and older than Bingo had been when she was brought to Potter Park, Tombi was still a baby elephant at about two years old, weighing 400 pounds and standing three feet, four inches tall. Being

Shipping an elephant takes a little more packaging than UPS could provide. Tombi was transferred from truck to exhibit in a wooden crate lifted by a large crane (photo courtesy Potter Park Zoo).

an African elephant, she looked very different from Bingo, as well. Tombi had much larger ears, her head had a different shape to it, and she was also destined to become a much larger adult.

Some of the keepers, still not over their grief from the loss of Bingo, took time to warm up to Tombi. When the new elephant arrived, keeper Nancy Harger said, "She's not as pretty as Bingo." With a little prompting, however, Harger relented, "She is a cute little scutter, isn't she?"[12]

One advantage that Tombi had over Bingo was that when she arrived, she had an elephant exhibit and decent indoor, winter shelter all ready for her to move into. In addition to this, the keepers had

After exiting her crate, Tombi takes a while to get used to her new surroundings (photo courtesy Potter Park Zoo).

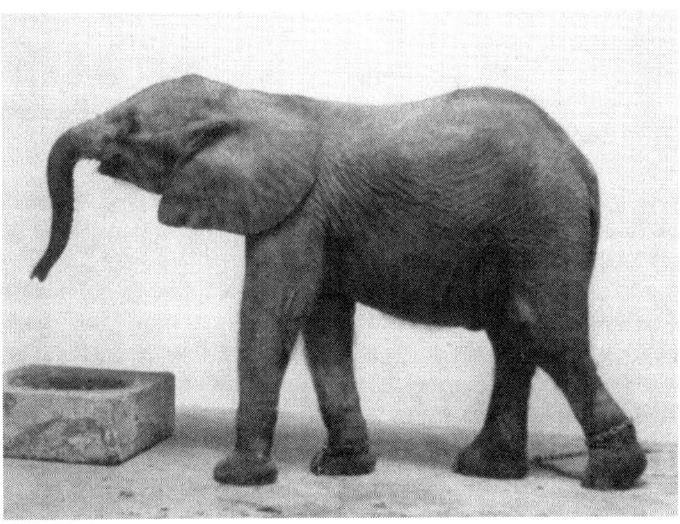

Not a cutie? There was some prejudice among keepers about Tombi because they missed Bingo so much, but there's no denying she was an adorable baby elephant (photo courtesy Potter Park Zoo).

learned a great deal about elephants from Bingo. However, they knew there was much more to learn. Bruce Snyder and the others were well aware of an elephant's dietary needs, but what they still lacked was sufficient training on how to manage such a large mammal.

The zoo decided to hire an expert on elephant handling: Herb Malzacher, from Madison, Wisconsin. Under his supervision, Potter Park Zoo keepers Bruce Snyder, Earl Austin, and later Mary Anne McNamara and Dave Dickert, learned how to teach Tombi to become used to her restraining chain at night and how to take guidance from her keepers. Snyder and Austin, in an effort to have Tombi become familiar and comfortable with them, would sit for hours with the young elephant, talking to her in calm voices and getting acquainted.

Target Training

Although the keepers at Potter Park Zoo did not do much in the way of training with Bingo, that changed considerably with Tombi. They employed a method now common in zoos called "target training." Target training is used for various reasons, including to train animals to accept medication or to move them from one exhibit area to another. Much safer than drugging an animal with a dart gun or forcefully moving it by other means, target training also causes much less stress on an animal. It is a method that requires the keeper to develop a relationship of human-animal trust, which is one of the most time-consuming parts of the process. Once an animal gains trust in a person (usually simply by the keeper spending a considerable amount of time with the animal so that it knows it is not under any threat), the trainer/keeper begins to modify the behavior of the animal. The keeper uses a "target," such as a short pole with a ball on the end of it, to draw the animal's attention to a specific task. When a task is done correctly, a food treat is offered; when the animal does not do something correctly, no reward is given. There is *definitely* no punishment of any kind! Trainers often combine the treat with a sound, such as a clicker, which the animal then associates with good behavior and a reward. Using target training, keepers at Potter Park Zoo were able to get Tombi to easily accept a safety chain at night without danger to her or her trainers.

With the cold Michigan winter over, Tombi was ready to spend time in the outdoor exhibit area in the spring of 1980. She instantly drew "oohs" and "ahhs" from zoo visitors. Like Bingo, she grew up quickly. After just two years at the zoo, Tombi weighed a full ton; by

Zoo keeper Earl Austin works with the adult Tombi in 1989. Some visitors objected to the chain that was used to keep the elephant and her trainers safe (photo courtesy Mary Anne McNamara).

1986 her weight was nearly 3,000 pounds; and by 1989 she was two tons of impressive mammalian heft. Just for fun, the Zoo Society held contests in which youngsters would try to guess Tombi's weight. Kids were also allowed to enter the elephant exhibit, ask questions about Tombi, and pet her. For this exercise, Tombi had been trained to lie on one side on command so that the children could easily reach her side and find out firsthand what an elephant's hairy hide felt like to the touch.

CHANGES AT THE ZOO MEAN SAYING "ADIEU"

Tombi proved to be almost as popular at Potter Park Zoo as Bingo had been, even though the local children did not have as much a feeling of "ownership" of the African elephant. She continued to live a healthy life for several years at Potter Park, but changing philosophies and increased knowledge of elephant care in zoos would eventually pressure the staff to come to a hard decision. Tombi would have to leave.

After Potter Park Zoo became accredited in 1986, it came under increasing scrutiny from the American Association of Zoos and Aquariums (AZA). By the late 1980s, the AZA and zoologists believed strongly that elephants should not live alone in isolation. In order for a zoo to maintain an elephant exhibit, therefore, they were required to own a minimum of two elephants.

A critical reason for this guideline was that young elephants, being social animals that lived in herds, needed to learn from older elephants in their groups how to behave like an elephant. Because Tombi lived by herself, she was not receiving this education, which would mean that if she were not introduced to others of her kind soon, she would never be able to live harmoniously with other elephants.

Doug Finley, zoo director at the time, explained the situation in a *Lansing State Journal* article: "It is critical that we attempt to social-

By the time Tombi reached adulthood, attitudes about keeping large pachyderms were changing. Elephants need lots of space and the company of other elephants, and so zoo director Doug Finley felt that Tombi would be much happier at the Indianapolis Zoo (photo courtesy Potter Park Zoo).

ize Tombi, and the longer this is delayed, the more difficult and dangerous it becomes. The longer we put off the relocation, the less chance we have of her successful transition into a group setting."[13]

Finley elaborated:

> The cost for keepers for the kind of infrastructure [needed to sustain a healthy elephant population of several animals] and the drain it was going to take on everything else [was not worth it].... The science wasn't behind us having an elephant at Potter Park. The weather conditions meant it needed to be put inside all winter. We had to put a chain around its leg all winter because it was so big we couldn't get in there and feed it and clean out the stall without having to chain it up. It just wasn't in my science or my ethics. It took a long time to convince everybody that this was a good decision, and there were still people, especially internally, who resented that move.[14]

After about a year of debating the issue, the decision was made: Tombi would be sent to the Indianapolis Zoo in 1989. She would still be owned, officially, by Potter Park Zoo, but she would now be able to live with others of her kind in a larger exhibit. After she was moved to Indianapolis, keepers there could indeed see the effects of her early solitary life. "Tombi is so meek she still doesn't know how to be an elephant," said one of the staff there in 1992.[14] The constant exposure to other elephants eventually improved Tombi's social skills, however, and she also received art therapy: keepers taught Tombi how to use a paintbrush, an activity that zoo staffs around the country have found elephants often enjoy.

Eventually, Potter Park Zoo sold Tombi outright, so that she no longer belongs to the City of Lansing. It is very unlikely, too, that the zoo will ever attempt to have elephants again, certainly not in the near future.

The experience of keeping Bingo and Tombi was a very educational one for all concerned at Potter Park Zoo. It taught both the staff and the zoo's visitors that even though getting to see a live elephant up close is thrilling, it is not always in the best interest of the animal. Zoos around the country have been coming to this same conclusion. For example, Detroit Zoo director Ron Kagan made the decision in 2005 that its two aging female elephants were better off living in a California sanctuary than within the confines of their exhibit, even though the Detroit exhibit was considered a fairly good one. Elephants require a great deal of space in order to move around and remain healthy; they also do best when they have contact with many others of their own kind.

Potter Park Zoo had learned some valuable lessons, indeed, and the 1980s would see many more changes at Lansing's zoo that were a reflection of changing times in zoo management around the country, as well as the progress Potter Park was making toward becoming a modern-day zoo.

5

The Master Plan

Activity at Potter Park Zoo peaked in the mid-1970s, with attendance soaring to nearly half a million visitors per year, exhibit construction progressing well with the help of the Friends, and hundreds of fascinating animals for visitors to see and enjoy. But along with this good news, new problems began to plague the park in that decade: vandalism, loitering, drugs, and even animal cruelty at the hands of trespassers. All of these troubles eventually climaxed in a deadly shooting at the pavilion outside the zoo.

Bad Behavior

Among the crimes perpetrated at the zoo by unwanted visitors were the thefts of several of its animals. In 1972, for example, a person or persons entered the grounds and stole a pheasant and an otter; in 1975, someone stole a sheep from the farmyard area. Typically, the extent of abuse of animals at the zoo by people had been limited to the occasional throwing of cans or stones. However, one of the worst cases came on January 4, 1977, when vandals entered the zoo and created some unforgivable mayhem. Two penguins, a raccoon, and a chicken were gone, other animals had been released from their exhibits. Worst of all, the criminals had taken boards with nails in them and repeatedly struck three white-tailed fawns. Fortunately, the deer later recovered, but the missing animals were likely dead, the raccoon certainly so, seeing as a pool of blood was discovered in the raccoon's cage. It was later learned that the raccoon had been killed when it was thrown repeatedly against a rock, and then skinned.

"I can't imagine what kind of person would do this," horrified zoo supervisor Jerry Miller said in disbelief.[1] Miller noticed that the vandals had deliberately selected those animals that had the most meat on them, as if they were harvesting zoo animals for food. A few days after the animal abuse was discovered, two teenagers from the town of Webberville were arrested in connection to the crime.

Meanwhile, the Fenner Arboretum was experiencing similar problems, as Lansing City Councilman John Anas could attest to after being robbed there one day. Illegal activity in the parks system was nothing new, of course. Crime had been noticeably increasing since the Great Depression, but it began to escalate precipitously in the 1970s. There were a number of possible reasons for the crowd problems at Potter Park Zoo—which may have been compounded when Michigan raised its drinking age from eighteen to twenty-one in 1978—while a dwindling parks security force could not keep up with public misbehavior.

Because of a decreasing budget, the number of part- and full-time security staff in the parks system had dropped considerably in 1977. This minimal staff was responsible for 104 parks within the city limits, not just the zoo and arboretum, which obviously meant not many security personnel were around to monitor trespassers. Compounding the problem was that these people were paid abysmally low salaries of about $3 per hour, resulting in a high turnover rate and a number of parks watchmen who were less than enthusiastic about their jobs. Reporter Mike Hughes noted that some watchmen "have looked the other way during trouble and have failed to tell anyone they weren't going to work."[2]

In response to the animal killings, parks department director Doug Finley said he would approach the City Council and ask for one full-time and one part-time zoo security guard. The city eventually responded, however, by integrating the separate parks force into the city's regular police force in February of 1979. By that time, there were only eight parks security people left under the direct control of the Parks Department, so there was little left to integrate.

Such measures did nothing to alleviate Potter Park Zoo's increasing security problems, however. And matters were about to get even worse.

AN END TO OPEN ACCESS TO THE ZOO

From the time of its founding and into the early 1980s, Potter Park Zoo was completely open to the public. Indeed, the zoo was not considered a separate entity from the park grounds, but rather more of an integrated feature of interest. Parking and admission were free, and there were no gates to the zoo and no large fences as there are today. Visitors could drive their cars onto the zoo grounds and all around the dirt trails that led to the exhibits. They could even park their cars within a few feet of the buildings, if they wished. As visitor numbers increased dramatically through the 1970s, this became a real problem. It was therefore decided to block off vehicle access to the zoo grounds with some fencing, which effectively created a loop from the entrance at Pennsylvania Avenue up to the parking lot by the zoo, and back out again. Interestingly, it was the budget for the fencing that determined once and for all how large the zoo grounds within Potter Park were to be: The city provided just so much money for the barrier, which was enough to enclose nineteen acres; thus, that is the size of the zoo today. The fence also had the psychological effect of making the zoo a separate entity from the park.

Teenagers and other young park users decided that this created an ideal area for cruising and hanging out during the summer months. Loitering, partying, blaring music, drinking, and drug use—mostly marijuana—plagued Potter Park to the point where families who wished to visit the zoo were being driven away by the sight of drunken and unruly crowds of young people. Rumors that a huge pot party was going to be held in April 1980 at the park led Mayor Gerald Graves to close the zoo and park. It was only one of a string of enforced closures in which police would cruise the area in beefed-up numbers, making several arrests. Fortunately, the mayor's action put a big damper on the pot party plans, and no one showed up for it.

In 1979, Mayor Graves and Parks Department Director Doug Finley proposed that a small parking fee of one dollar per vehicle would put an end to the problem. However, the City Council was reluctant to start charging fees because it would be an unpopular decision with many voters. Some of the Council members even went as far as to say that a fee would be unfair because it would not be affordable to some, while residents near the park fretted that neighborhood streets would fill with cars as people parked in front of their houses to avoid the fee.

Opposition quickly crumbled after the shooting.

On July 6, 1980, a young man was shot dead while exiting the Pavilion building in the park. Doug Finley addressed the City Council that day on the issue and obtained immediate approval for the parking fee. At first, the City Council declared that the dollar-per-vehicle fee would only be temporary, but by the next year it had become permanent, with money going to such projects as pothole repair for the parking lot. Taking an idea that was used at the Ingham County Fair to control crowds, the City also hired a part-time mounted policeman, Sergeant Ray Rahall, to patrol the parking lot from Wednesday through Sunday, the zoo's busiest times. Sergeant Rahall and his horse, Tarrz, together known as the "Mountie Patrol," quickly became favorites at the zoo, where children would run to greet and pet the horse gleefully.

The difference at the zoo and park before and after the fee was initiated was like night and day. The rowdies, unwilling to shell out a buck for their previously free party grounds, immediately stopped hanging out at the park, and visitors to the zoo felt safer seeing the clearly visible mounted policeman riding about. Rahall was later joined by another mounted officer, Dave Henderson, and his horse, Ms. Strawberry Reid.

Fears that fees would drive away legitimate zoo visitors were dispelled. Hundreds of cars visited Potter Park Zoo each weekend, carrying families perfectly willing to pay a dollar to find a quiet, secure place to spend the day, free of vagrants. The Friends encouraged families to return to their zoo, too, by sponsoring special events like "Family Fun Day" after the fee was employed. During the cruising days of hot rods and pot smokers, over 800 cars were entering the park *per hour* just to cruise and make noise; that number decreased to about 400 cars a day, but these were paying guests who wanted to enjoy Potter Park in peace and see the zoo animals. Furthermore, the concern that people would park on neighborhood streets and walk to the zoo also proved completely groundless. Michiganders are drivers, not walkers.

Despite the seeming success of the fee, there were still lingering protests about it. A Potter Park Citizen's Advisory Committee was formed to urge City Council to withdraw the fee, but such opposition groups were in the minority.

This is not to say that the parking fee and better security solved all the zoo's problems. The grounds were still fairly easy for intruders to access, and occasionally criminals still did so with malevolent intent. In September 1986, for example, one of the worst crimes to take place at Potter Park Zoo occurred when at least one, and probably more, trespassers jumped two fences to enter the horse exhibit. Here they found Maryland, a three-foot-tall, fifteen-year-old miniature horse that was a gift from an MSU veterinarian. Using bottles and a knife, the attackers struck and stabbed the little mare repeatedly. She was found bleeding and depressed the next day. The staff treated the wound and gave her pain killers, noticing visible bruising around the vagina. Later, they noticed the uterine wall had been perforated, and they were treating this problem when she died four days later of peritonitis.

Aghast at such cruelty, police could only guess that the killers were copying an earlier attack on animals at the Saginaw Children's Zoo.

Such menacing behavior, while extremely troubling and baffling, would occur every now and then at Potter Park over the coming years. However, it was much more rare for animal abuse to be perpetrated at the hands of outsiders, thanks to the new fee and security measures at the zoo.

DAWN OF THE 1980S: NEW AVIARY AND WOLF EXHIBIT

With an almost audible collective sigh of relief, zoo supervisor Jerry Miller and Parks Department Director Doug Finley felt they could focus their attentions back on the zoo itself and away from the worry of unruly crowds. The Friends of the Zoo had done a lot to help bring Potter Park around, lending it a new energy and community involvement that had revitalized the zoo. The Friends were still accomplishing a great deal in the early 1980s. For example, they helped raise funds for a new grey wolf exhibit, which opened in 1981. The wolves, which had previously been kept in a concrete pen, now had a natural setting full of trees, bushes, and an artificial den, compliments of labor donated by the Youth Conservation Corps.

Another addition to the exhibits was a brand-new free-flight aviary, which debuted in the fall of 1981. As with the wolf exhibit, it was high-spirited volunteer helpers who made the aviary affordable for the zoo. "If we had contracted (to private interests) the aviary construction," zoo supervisor Miller pointed out, "it would have cost about $60,000. Instead, it will only cost about $30,000."[3] Design fees were generously waived by local architect Morris Stein, and the Friends raised well over a thousand dollars for the structure as well.

The wolf exhibit was designed to mimic the natural habitat of timber wolves as closely as possible (photo by Bruce Bolender courtesy of the Potter Park Zoo Society).

Labor and materials were brought in by Blissner and Son Construction Company and the Walter Neller Company, with additional help from zoo staff and volunteers. Keepers worked weekends without pay, as did assistant supervisor Bill Swix and volunteers such as Sonny Lumbert.

When they were done, the aviary was state of the art for its time. It included a waterfall, stream, and pond area, plenty of plants and trees donated by the Capitol Area Landscape Nurserymen's Association, and a winding path through the center of it all. Once completed, the aviary was stocked with various bird species, including a heron, wood ducks, vultures, and peacocks.

Also new in 1981 was a new species of animal called the crab-eating fox. The pair of foxes, which come from South America, were a gift from the National Zoo in Washington, D.C. The zoo also obtained a black leopard (or panther), which had been confiscated from a private owner who had kept it in violation of the Endangered Species Act.

THE MASTER PLAN

Despite the many accomplishments over the previous decade, the zoo lacked focus. Even more important, perhaps, was the increasingly

The free flight aviary—seen here as a model—provided a much more natural exhibit space for birds than the old Bird House. However, by 2007 it was showing its age. It had also been plagued by raccoons that had repeatedly broken in and killed birds, so it was torn down that year (photo courtesy Potter Park Zoo).

savvy public's insistence on better exhibits for the animals. The wolves may have had a new, natural exhibit, but many of the zoo's residents, including the bears, lions, and chimpanzee, were stuck in concrete quarters surrounded by stone walls or iron bars. What was needed, it was decided, was a Master Plan that would offer a clear vision of where the zoo was going and how its future would be realized.

Doug Finley, the director of Lansing's Department of Parks and Recreation, zoo supervisor Jerry Miller, and the Friends of the Zoo put their heads together and hired the architectural firm James H. Bassett, Inc., as well as the professional advice of zoologist Earl B. Wells, a former Lansing resident (and former Potter Park Zoo employee) who at the time was director of the Ft. Wayne Zoo. The "Master Plan for Redevelopment" was published in February 1984. It was an ambitious document.

The basic philosophy behind the Master Plan was that the exhibits should be redesigned in accordance with changing ideals at zoos around the world. Model zoological parks, such as the San Diego Zoo, had created outstanding exhibits that simulated as closely as

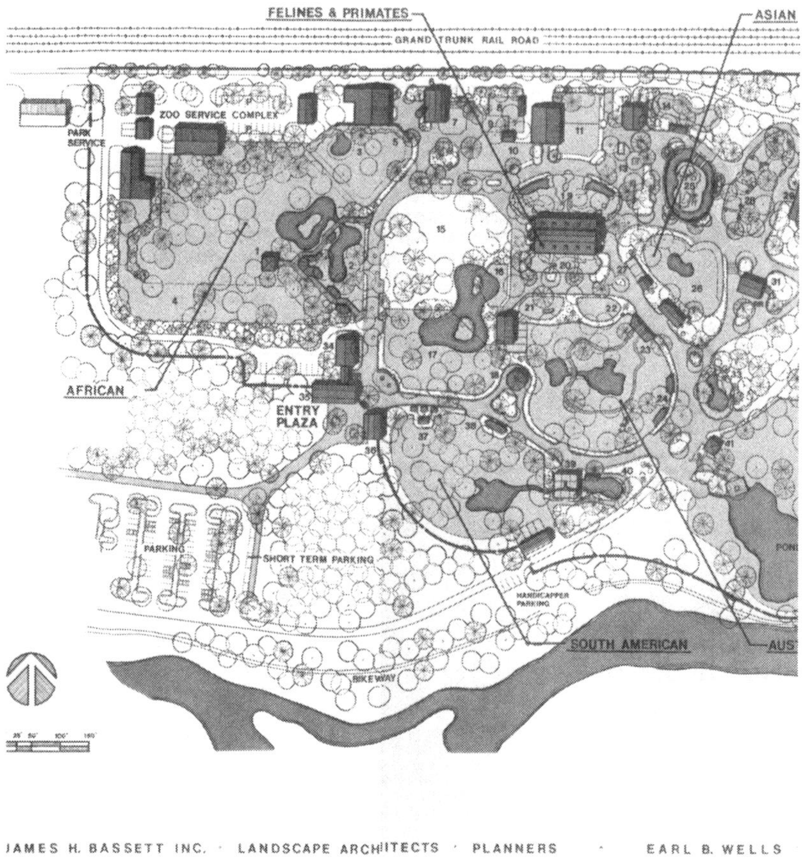

The original 1984 Master Plan was a highly ambitious plan for a zoo with chronic

possible the habitats to which their various animal species had become adapted. This not only created a more pleasing exhibit for visitors, but it proved beneficial to animals' physical and mental health and made it much more likely for them to breed, a fact that was especially significant for endangered species that were part of the Species Survival Plan.

The Species Survival Plan

Often described by zoo people as a "computer dating service for animals," the Species Survival Plan (SSP) was initiated in 1981 as a cooperative system between zoos in which the lineage of

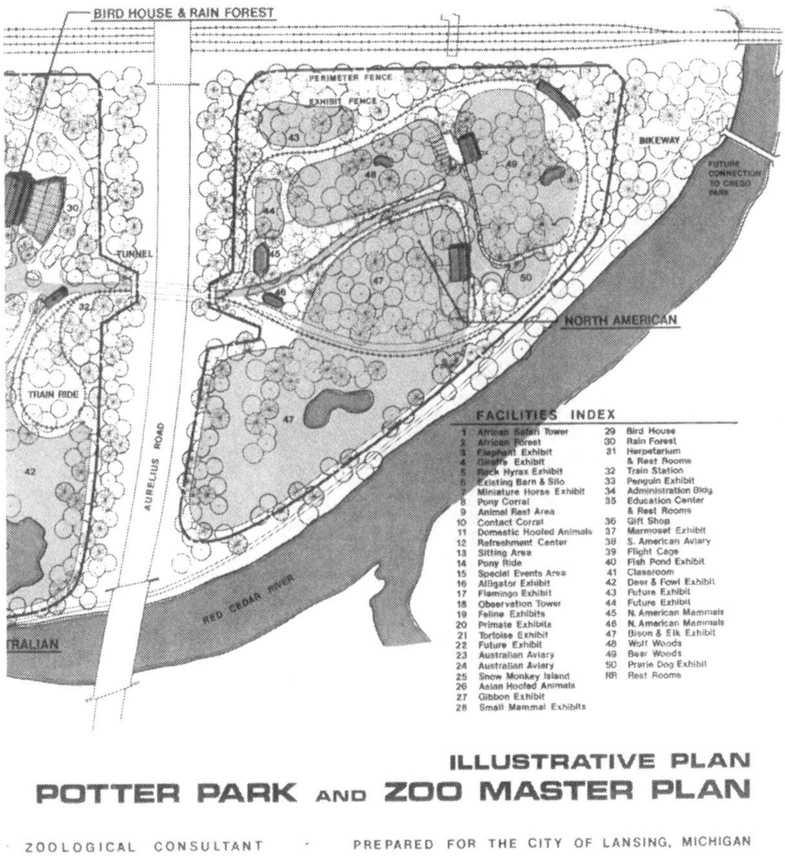

financial problems (courtesy Potter Park Zoo Society).

endangered animals is tracked and males and females are paired up based on the best genetic matches. Records of which zoos own which animals are maintained in the International Species Inventory System (ISIS), which was first developed by Dale Make and Dr. Ulysses Seal back in 1973. The SSP is designed to encourage genetic diversity in zoo animals, because if too much inbreeding (breeding between closely related animals) occurs, this can result in everything from still births to birth defects and susceptibility to disease. Because zoos now get the majority of their animals from either other zoos and sanctuaries or from animals that are born on the grounds, it is more important than ever that genetic diversity be monitored closely.

The Master Plan concept for the zoo's new entry plaza (photo courtesy Potter Park Zoo Society).

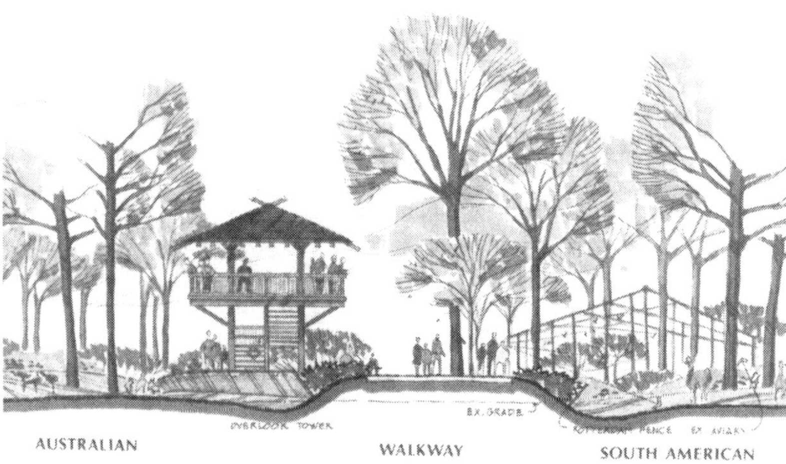

Potter Park Zoo wished to organize its exhibit by world region, as was the growing trend among zoos by the 1980s. The Master Plan included Australian and South American exhibits (photo courtesy Potter Park Zoo Society).

One of the most ambitious projects in the Master Plan was to expand the old Bird House to include a state-of-the-art rainforest exhibit (photo courtesy Potter Park Zoo Society).

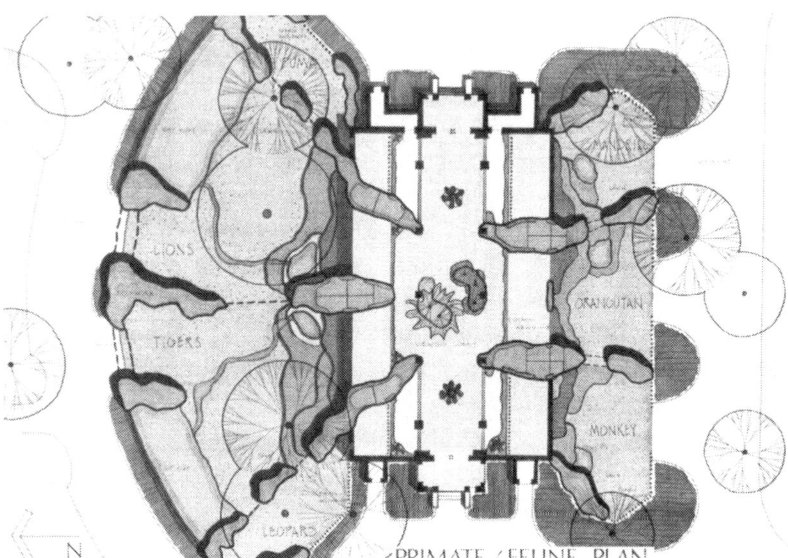

The redesign of the Feline/Primate House was one of the few projects of the first Master Plan to see the light of day (photo courtesy Potter Park Zoo Society).

Species Survival Plan signs are posted around the zoo to indicate which animals are endangered and part of the AZA's organized breeding program (photo by Kevin Hile).

The plan developed by James H. Bassett, Inc. was both impressive and ambitious. It took into account accommodations for the four main focuses of all modern zoos: recreation, conservation, education, and research. In all of Potter Park's previous history, it had mainly managed to fulfill only the first of these goals. By the early 1980s, it was only just beginning to develop education programs, while its conservation role had been fairly minimal, since many of its animals had been surplus specimens from other zoos, or, occasionally, animals found in the wild or purchased from animal dealers. Research, other than perhaps what was learned by MSU vets treating the zoo's animals, had been nonexistent.

Creating more natural habitats for the animals would go a long way toward satisfying all these goals because improved space would encourage the animals to behave more naturally.

The Master Plan not only transformed the outdated exhibits, many dating back a half century or more, but it also increased the size of the zoo to twenty-nine acres by expanding the grounds eastward to the other side of Aurelius Road (Aurelius had once only reached Mt. Hope

Avenue south of the zoo, but had been extended past the zoo and north to I-496 in 1971). This eastern addition alone would add seven acres to the wildlife park. Another four acres were to be added to the existing grounds adjacent to the park. The two sides would be connected by a train route that ran through a tunnel beneath Aurelius Road. Restoring a train ride to the zoo was a popular notion, but this train would have taken a completely different route. With a station near the Aurelius tunnel, it would loop by the deer and waterfowl exhibit, then through the tunnel to the new eastern addition, which would be the North American region to include wolves, bison, bears, and a prairie dog exhibit.

The rest of the zoo would also be reorganized according to continents, with new Asian, Australian, African, and South American exhibits. The old moats behind the Bird House would be completely renovated to create a brand new enclosed Rain Forest exhibit. A herpetarium would be built, along with a new penguin exhibit surrounded by glass for underwater viewing opportunities, and Monkey Island would be redesigned as a snow monkey exhibit complete with a waterfall and underground service access area. Also up for renovation was the malodorous Feline/Primate House, which would be redesigned inside and out, adding an outdoor area for the primates and improving the areas for lions and tigers.

Furthermore, new never-before-seen species at Potter Park would be added, including alligators, rock hyrax, black swans, orangutans, mandrills, giraffes, flamingoes, and of course the penguins, Japanese snow monkeys, and prairie dogs.

Finally, new concession stands would be built, as well as a new entry plaza.

The philosophy behind the Master Plan was never to create a megazoo to rival the likes of Detroit or San Diego, but rather to conceive the best imaginable small zoo possible that would benefit both the animals and the zoo's visitors.

Just one look at this plan and anyone could see a major flaw: money. The Master Plan was estimated to cost at least $5 million to realize, and another $1 million was desired for renovations to the surrounding park. Where would the money come from?

TIME TO GET SERIOUS ABOUT BIG BUCKS

Since the early 1970s, the Friends of the Zoo had contributed about $500,000 to Potter Park Zoo for exhibit improvements. While this had made a big difference and was much appreciated, such a fund-raising pace would never suffice to make the Master Plan a reality. There was only one thing to do to set the Master Plan in motion, Parks Director Doug Finley knew: go to the voters. The idea was not to seek a millage, but to try for a $1.5 million bond issue.

Seeking a special city tax for the zoo was an idea that had been tried in the 1960s, only to fail, so Finley was nervous that a bond issue would see resistance. The Friends of the Zoo and the zoo staff had more confidence that Lansing would support them, however. In May 1984, the City Council approved putting the issue to the voters. Finley got to work by organizing a campaign to promote the ballot proposal, which would raise $1.5 million for the first stages of the Master Plan.

Spending about $5,000, Finley had informational materials printed and mailed to absentee voters and certain other targeted neighborhoods that seemed critical for the vote. Working many hours to promote the ballot issue, the campaign paid off when the August election brought great news: 6,955 voters approved the bond issue, with only 2,602 voting against. "I don't think we expected it would pass by that great a majority," Friends president Ellen Lumbert confessed at the time, "but we're delighted it did."[4]

In retrospect, Finley said, asking for $1.5 million for the zoo had been a mistake: "If we made one mistake, it was not asking for enough money. We only asked for enough money to do the Lion House" and begin on the Master Plan. "We should have asked for more money, but we were concerned that we weren't going to have the support…. We could have asked for twice that much money and had the ability to do a lot of things. That then capped us for about five years … because the bond had to be paid off within a five-year period, so we couldn't go back on the ballot again right away."[5]

With $1.5 million guaranteed for the zoo, the other $3.5 million would have to come from somewhere else. Finley hoped that further private donations would make up for lost ground, but the zoo was never able to win enough financial support in this way to make up such a large difference. It seemed, then, that everyone would have to make do, at least for the time being, with what they had.

Chilling Out: Time for Penguins!

Though it appeared that progress on the Master Plan would have to proceed at a turtle's, rather than a hare's pace, everyone was eager to give the city of Lansing *something* for their support as soon as possi-

Potter Park Zoo has, over the years, featured many exhibits displaying North American animals, such as this barn owl, that have been very popular. Zoo animals do not always have to be exotic to be educational and interesting! (photo by Bruce Cornelius).

ble. A barn owl exhibit was opened early in 1986, but the zoo's leaders understood that the public was looking for a little more splash for their buck. It was therefore decided that the first big project after the passage of the bond issue would be a brand new penguin exhibit. The Friends held fund-raising events in June of that year to supplement the money coming from the bond issue, and by late-summer a state-of-the-art outdoor penguin enclosure had been constructed, complete with temperature-controlled water, nesting areas, and indoor quarters surrounded by gunite rocks to make the area look natural.

"The improvements are part of new zoological efforts to house animals in environments similar to their natural habitats," noted Leona Ison in a *Lansing State Journal* article.[6]

"Penguin" Is a Peculiar Name

When I was a docent at the Detroit Zoo, I was told that the word "penguin" came from a type of hat popular among English gentlemen in the eighteenth century. Explorers from England, chancing upon their first penguins, fancied that the bird resembled the hat, hence the name. Upon deeper research, however, I learned that "penguin" more likely dates back to the year 1578, when it was coined by combining the Welsh words "pen" for head and "gwyn" for white, and applied to the Great Auk, a North Atlantic aquatic bird hunted to extinction in the seventeenth century. When sailors later came upon today's penguins, they applied the old word to a new bird. Let us hope that the fate that befell the Great Auk does not repeat itself with the penguins of today.

When people think of penguins, what usually comes to mind are emperor, king, or macaroni penguins, but there are fifteen other penguin species as well (some scientists say fourteen, depending on how the species are differentiated). At the time, it happened that the Detroit Zoo had just received a large shipment of Magellanic penguins that had been caught in the wild. Magellanics are a good choice for a Michigan zoo because their natural habitat along the coast of Chile is similar in many ways—though somewhat drier—to the American Midwest's climate. Keepers Bruce Snyder and Jenny Rentfrow traveled to the Cleveland Zoo to work with the penguins there first, so that they would gain some experience before the birds were brought to Lansing. Then they went to the Detroit Zoo to select penguins for the new exhibit. "I remember going down to Detroit [where they had just received wild-caught penguins].... And they said, 'Pick

Keepers Bruce Snyder and Jenny Rentfrow introduce penguins to their new exhibit. The penguin exhibit opened in 1986 to much fanfare. It was the first major exhibit to open after the bond issue was passed (photo courtesy Mary Anne McNamara).

out which penguins you want.' We had no clue which ones we wanted. We went in there and we just started grabbing penguins. It was pretty funny!"[7]

Unfortunately, four of the eighteen penguins brought in from Detroit perished from aspergillosis. This is a common respiratory disease that many penguins contract. It is caused by a fungus that occurs naturally in the environment. Penguins are exposed to it through breathing; normally, this does not cause any problems, except when a bird is stressed or immune-compromised in some way. Usually, the fungus remains fairly dormant and the disease is considered chronic and not dangerous. However, when penguins become stressed for any reason, the condition can be aggravated to the point of being lethal.

The new penguin exhibit debuted on July 20, 1986, when the remaining fourteen Magellanic penguins were released into the enclosure in an event heavily covered by the media. The keepers had given the penguins all names (Greta, Sparty, Jumper, etc.), but one, Pete the Penguin, became a celebrity at Potter Park. Longtime zoo

A Magellanic penguin. There are over a dozen species of penguins in the world, many of which, like the Magellanic, actually live in temperate climates (photo by Bruce Bolender courtesy of the Potter Park Zoo Society).

friend Jim Hough praised the new addition to the zoo, adding proudly: "You may not have noticed it, but Potter Park Zoo has quietly become this city's No. 1 attraction—more than half a million visitors each year. Not even MSU football can match that."[8]

Lansing Mayor Terry McKane made a telling observation on opening day for the penguins, too: "Potter Park Zoo is a perfect example of what government and community can do together. If this project had been left to government alone, it would have failed or fallen far short of expectations. The zoo society and all of the community involvement are what made this project work."[9]

Within a few months, the penguins clearly began to relax. How was this known? Why, because they started laying eggs! The first eggs were seen in March 1987. However, the initial clutches did not hatch successfully. The next year, Potter Park Zoo had its first successful penguin hatchlings: two chicks. A clear sign that the exhibit was a comfortable place for the penguins to thrive. Despite extensive planning, however, some mistakes were made. The barriers surrounding the exhibit were not quite high enough. Penguins are capable of jumping quite high out of the water. Perhaps the exhibit designers did not believe that the pool was large enough for the penguins to get a good swimming start, but it was apparently just adequate for several of them to leap out and over the barrier. Penguins were seen one day waddling their merry way toward the keeper parking lot at the back of the zoo near Aurelius Road. They were quickly rounded up, and the exhibit hours had to be shortened so that the keeper staff could watch that the birds did not escape again. Soon, though, the exhibit was modified to put an end to such mischievous explorations.

LE PIÈCE DE RESISTANCE: ACCREDITATION

There is no doubt that the true testimony that Potter Park Zoo was on the right track came in 1986, when the little Lansing zoo was first accredited by the American Association of Zoos and Aquariums (AZA), which in the mid-1980s was known as the American Association of Zoological Parks and Aquariums (AAZPA). While zoos across the country still needed to be licensed by the U.S. Department of Agriculture in order to continue operating, the AZA had taken over much of the role from the federal government for assuring that zoos maintained quality exhibits and cared for the animal species that resided within them. This meant not only that the animals had enough food, water, shelter, and medical care, but that all other steps possible were being taken to ensure their well-being, including their psychological and social health. The emphasis here is especially on the keepers and other zoo staff to maintain a high level of professionalism at all times, which the Potter Park Zoo staff had accomplished.

The Association of Zoos and Aquariums

Founded in 1924, the American Association of Zoological Parks and Aquariums was organized by a group of zoological garden directors and operated as part of the American Institute of Park Executives. Later transferred under the auspices of the National Recreation and Parks Association in 1966, the AAZPA broke away and became an independent organization. Now known as the Association of Zoos and Aquariums, the AZA is considered the overseeing body of all zoos and aquariums in the United States. It regularly monitors the quality of care of zoo animals throughout the country, inspecting each facility once every five years. Over the years, these inspections have become more and more rigorous, as more demands are made on zoos, including everything from medical care and exhibit improvements to record keeping and education. Zoos that pass the inspection process become accredited and are allowed to participate in SSP programs. Those that do not are typically given a year in order to comply with any areas in which they have fallen short. This has often happened at Potter Park Zoo, but the Lansing zoo has always managed to correct any shortcomings to be accredited.

In addition to inspections, which ensure quality zoos, the AZA has also helped foster an atmosphere of greater cooperation among zoos. Especially prior to the 1970s, there was always a kind of competitive spirit among zoos in the United States. This may have caused each zoo to strive to be better than others, but it also resulted in preventing the sharing of information and animals, which would have benefited them all. Today, zoos all across America—and, indeed, the world—recognize that they share the missions of education, conservation, and science, and that partnership is the name of the game.

At the time it was first accredited, Potter Park Zoo was one of the smallest zoos in the country to achieve this important status (only about one in ten wildlife parks in the United States are accredited). Significantly, AZA accreditation meant that the zoo was now given the green flag to care for some of the world's most endangered species. Before this, Potter Park Zoo had always carried a fairly interesting array of wildlife, including a chimpanzee, spider monkeys, and lions, but as these animals became increasingly rare in the wild, it would be impossible for the zoo to keep such species without AZA approval.

It was a great milestone for Potter Park Zoo. It marked yet another new era for Lansing's zoo that was about to charge in like a raging lion, changing the landscape of the zoo forever and altering its very character in revolutionary ways. But revolutions can be upsetting times, and there were, indeed, many people who were upset by what was to come. In retrospect, one can see that the changes were needed, though perhaps painful.

6

Growing Pains: Becoming a Modern Zoo

The months that followed the opening of the penguin exhibit and accreditation for the zoo portended great changes to come. Jerry Miller announced in July 1986 that the next big renovation/construction project would be the long-awaited revamping of the outdated and sometimes maligned Feline/Primate House. That was the good news; the bad news was that during the next couple of years the building would be closed. This meant that zoo fans would have to bid farewell to some of Potter Park's beloved animals, including the African lions Butch and Sunnie, who had been born at the zoo to much fanfare and were sent to the drive-through Buena Vista Zoo near Springfield, Missouri. The spider monkeys, however, would benefit quickly with a brand new exhibit that would open in the summer of 1987.

The Feline/Primate House: The First Major Renovation

It would not be unfair to say that everyone at the Potter Park Zoo—keepers, administrators, and guests alike—were excited about having the Feline/Primate House remodeled. The cavernous, stark, and, yes, somewhat forbidding building resembled a prison more than a friendly home for lions, tigers, white-handed gibbons, and other species which were confined to ten-foot by ten-foot or ten-foot by twenty-foot spaces. The floors were concrete, which made them easy for keepers to clean, but they were little more sophisticated than garages. Even though the lions and other feline species (which changed from year to year) had outdoor spaces, they were not much better than what was inside; the primates were completely out of luck in this regard, lacking any outdoor quarters whatsoever.

The architectural plans for the renovation were impressive and would prove appealing not only to zoo visitors, but to the animals as well. Inside, the space would be designed to have an indoor simulated garden, complete with a miniature waterfall. The iron railings between the enclosures and the guests would be removed, allowing visitors to walk right next to the animals' quarters. Between animals and people would be a four-inch thick wall made of two kinds of

The original interior of the Feline/Primate House was old school. Concrete enclosures made the exhibits easy to clean, but they were not in the least natural, resembling more of a prison than a modern zoo (photo courtesy Potter Park Zoo).

The renovated interior of the Feline/Primate House is welcoming and much more natural. The improvements to the building also included the outdoor exhibits, adding enclosures to the south side and improving the north side areas (photo by Bruce Bolender courtesy of the Potter Park Zoo Society).

glass to allow easy viewing and eliminate the jail-like bars. The floor inside would be carpeted, with both stairs and a ramp to make everything accessible to people with or without physical challenges.

Outside, both the north and south areas adjacent to the building would become outdoor exhibits for felines and primates, with the enclosure including full landscaping, running water, and interesting rocks or trees to climb on.

Once again, Lansing area residents could be counted upon to do more than their expected share. Although the zoo had the $1.5 million it needed for the Feline/Primate House renovation, thanks to the bond issue, some people wanted to make absolutely certain that the animals would get the very best of everything. One of these people was Harold Gross, a pioneer in Lansing radio who founded its first station, WJIM-AM, in 1934. WJIM would later expand into television to become Lansing's second TV station in 1952. "I'd like to see the zoo rise to state and national prominence," Gross explained when he gave Potter Park $100,000 toward the renovation.[1]

Additional help came from volunteers, who donated their time, muscle, and supplies to the project, including the Granger Construction Company, which provided the zoo with reduced fees toward the building of the Feline/Primate House.

Donations also rolled in for the new spider monkey exhibit, including from the Lansing chapter of Women in Construction and the Oldsmobile Supervisors Council.

As 1987 arrived, the spider monkey exhibit was on track, everything was a "go" for the Feline/Primate House—though the cost estimate quickly rose an additional $200,000—and the zoo added a dromedary camel ride as a fun diversion for guests. However, the zoo would lose two very important people: Ellen and Sonny Lumbert. Ellen, who had served as the Friends of the Zoo president since 1974, and Sonny, who had managed much of the business end for the organization, officially announced in the newspaper they would be leaving Potter Park Zoo to go into the restaurant business, though Ellen had already stepped down as president the year before. In their honor, the classroom building next to the pond was renamed the Lumbert Education Center. Unfortunately, when a new education center was completed in 2000, the old sign on the Lumbert building was removed.

Things were changing at Potter Park Zoo, and for some those changes were to prove a bit uncomfortable. In retrospect, all parties concerned would come to agree that what would happen next behind the scenes at the zoo was a necessary change that resulted in a more professional organization; on the other hand, most also agree the transition could have been handled much better than it was.

After Ellen and Sonny left, the next to go would be zoo supervisor Jerry Miller and his loyal right-hand man, Bill Swix. There would be a new animal curator, Gerry Brady; and many other new faces as well. It might be said that the revolution that was to come was the result of Potter Park Zoo's own ambitions. Tremendous plans for multimillion dollar renovations could no longer be supported by the well-meaning, grass-roots style of fund raising that had been the hallmark of the Friends of the Zoo and that people like Art Mauk and Jim Hough had known. Master Plans required campaigning, politics, and major corporate sponsors.

It was a new era. But although one might be tempted to look back nostalgically at the days of the Friends, the time to come had its own heart and spirit as well. Potter Park Zoo was still a small, struggling zoo, and it would maintain the community spirit that had kept it alive. "I'd just like people to remember how Potter Park Zoo looked thirty years ago," said Ellen Lumbert philosophically, "and then what it looks like today. That's all. Great improvements have been made."[2]

Ellen remained on the new Zoo Society's Board of Directors during the transitional period before leaving for good.

One other salient change was that the Herman logo was no more. Perhaps it was too quaint and old-fashioned to endure the test of time, or perhaps it was no longer seen as a professional-looking emblem for the new Society, but the last visible remembrance of the once-famous Mexican burro was scrapped.

One person who would remember Herman especially fondly was Jerry Miller, who, along with Bill Swix, announced his retirement in July 1988. "One of the animals I really missed when he died was Herman the burro. Herm liked to sneak up behind you and bite you in the middle of the back, and then run like hell because he knew you were going to chew him out for it."[3]

Jerry looked back fondly on the accomplishments made while he was at Potter Park Zoo, including the barn owl exhibit, where five owls had been born over the years, raising a baby white-handed gibbon named Missy in his house after her mother had died, and the work they did with Bingo and Tombi. As for Bill, one of the animals who had a special place in his heart was Bo the tiger, who was at the zoo in the 1960s, when he first became a keeper. "He wasn't friendly to everyone, but he was to me,"[4] he recalled. One dark and stormy night in Lansing, a tree limb crashed through the roof of Bo's exhibit; Bill found the tiger shivering and crying like a cub, but the keeper's voice comforted the big cat, who trusted Bill enough to let him move him to other quarters.

Both Jerry and Bill could proudly declare that no keepers had received more than minor bites and scratches during their time there. Also, they had both been key figures in working to get the Feline/Primate House project started.

Miller, who would go on to own and operate his own llama farm, was only fifty-one when he left the zoo in 1988; Swix was fifty-two, leaving to work for Yunker Memorials. Both were not so advanced in years that they could not have stayed at Potter Park Zoo for many more years. But rumors abounded that shake ups in the Parks and Recreation Department in Lansing were causing many of the changes at the zoo. Doug Finley decided to step down from the director's post, taking a pay cut in the process, to become the new zoo manager in Miller's place.

Finley explained his career move: "In the late '70s and early '80s I spent a disproportional amount of energy on the zoo.... And at some point I finally felt like I wasn't doing a good enough job at my job because I was championing part of my job [the zoo] maybe more than I should have. And at that point I said to the mayor [Lansing Mayor Terry McKane] that I really want to see this through; I want to finish this job, and I'm a liability to you if I … don't pay the fullest attention to other issues like the city market, which was under the Parks and Recreation Department at the time." He added, "But it was a fun pay cut; it was the best pay cut I ever made."[5]

Doug Finley led the zoo from 1988 to 1992 (photo courtesy David Kenyon).

DOUG FINLEY: A CONTROVERSIAL LEADER

While Finley was enthusiastic about leading the zoo when he took over the director's job in 1988, many at the zoo were not fond of his style of leadership. The new zoo director felt that Potter Park Zoo was lagging behind other zoos in the country. Finley believed that the facilities for many of the animals were below par, especially for some of the larger residents, such as Tombi the elephant. It was his decision to close the exhibits behind the Bird/Reptile House. "The moving of Tombi was not the first [major decision]. We made a series of decisions and not one of those decisions was popular internally, but all of them needed to be done. I think the first week on the job I said we were closing the bear moats.... Think of how the public saw them as they stood there and saw these bears pacing back and forth.... So I said we're not going to do this." There were wolves and Arctic fox behind the Bird House at the time.

Finley felt that people would not support a zoo that kept animals under such conditions. "They cannot feel sorry for the animals that are in it," he insisted. "They cannot look at an animal and say this [looks like] punishment.... [We] needed them to support the zoo to raise the funds and make it better."

Admittedly, in his early years as parks director, Finley had not been too involved with the zoo, but that changed later in his administration because he came to see that the zoo had been allowed to deteriorate again "physically and operationally. It had good, good people.... The Lumberts [for example] were good people. Very hard working, very sincere, very honest people. But, yet again, each year you saw a problem that wasn't there the year before. [The zoo] was continuing to decline. Some of the things that were in that period [the late 1980s] were items that I didn't try to solve as an 'issue.' I tried to look at what was the core problem of what made the zoo sick, not what was the symptom of it being sick.... My concern was: Is the structure there? Is the vision there? Are the people in place who can take all these symptomatic issues and make them healthy again by addressing the bigger picture?"

In addition to removing some of the animals Finley felt should not be kept at the zoo, he wished to make improvements to the buildings and grounds. "I had a philosophy that every day, by the end of the day, even if it takes just five minutes, one thing we're going to do today was to make the zoo better. And if that was as simple as painting the flagpole, and that was it, then we made the zoo better by painting that flagpole. That was probably, in retrospect, something I shouldn't have done because there was a general feeling [among the staff] that any time we made an improvement it was a condemnation of the past, and some of those people had been there for so long that someone coming in and saying this isn't good enough was probably something I needed to be more diplomatic, but I put my emphasis on getting things done first."

Still, every act, large and small, that Finley accomplished at the zoo made a noticeable change. Even little things, such as adding thatched roofs to some of the structures to give them more of an African feel, or installing a new sign at the Pennsylvania Avenue entrance, gave the zoo a refreshing facelift—or, at least, a bit of a nip and tuck.

When Finley wasn't struggling with attitudes at the zoo itself, he was often at loggerheads with the Lansing City Council. Such problems had become the status quo for zoo administrators since Downey's time; they always found the Council's lack of financial support less than inspiring. Some former zoo directors have been uncomfortable talking about the political issue openly. Jerry Miller, for example, would only say that he found going to the City to beg for money just to keep the zoo buildings and infrastructure in good repair the least appealing part of his job. Finley put it this way:

> The money was never there, [or] coming in fast enough. A lot of competing things in government at that time [the late 1980s and early 1990s]. Still are. I'd love to be able to say that the City Council saw the value of the zoo and jumped behind it, but that's never been true.... I don't understand it. They'll put in $20 million to put in a ballpark downtown [Oldsmobile Park], [yet] the ballpark, even in its greatest projection on how many people it was going to draw, was never as much as Potter Park was already drawing. But yet again, they virtually wouldn't commit a dime outside of what was generated by admission fees and a few small appropriations out of the millage money.

A number of Council members had their own favorite projects, such as the river trail, while others remained largely indifferent to the zoo. It was not that they were against the zoo *per se,* so much as they were not greatly in favor of it. During Finley's involvement with the zoo, there were some in the Council who proved supportive. Among those he highlighted were Alfreda Schmidt, Lucille Belen, and Terry McKane. However, as is true in a democratic government, even if one could find supporters, they would eventually leave office.

Finley would leave the zoo, too, in 1992. “One of my regrets is that I always felt like I left the zoo too soon.... I always felt like it was a book with a page open, you know? You never quite finish the last chapter. It was a great book, you got through part of it, but you don’t know how it ever finished. I always feel that I probably missed something, because Potter Park meant so much. It still does. It is before the malls and before the ... cinemas. It was a place where families went. It’s a place where three, four generations of memories [are] that are so important as part of a family structure. It is a place to put people in contact ... with animals and learning experiences. It was—as best as we could afford—attractive, educational, humane.... It helps people understand the world around them. So many people have no idea what the world is outside their own urban community.”

In the short time that Doug Finley led Potter Park Zoo, he may not have won many fans, but he significantly changed the entire tone at the zoo. His approach was to always look forward toward improving the zoo, which may have rankled some of those who loved the park as it had been, but others would recognize the necessary change. Another important contribution he made was to view zoo management not only with regard to park visitors, but also through a much more scientific perspective. This was reflected in his deep concern for appropriate animal exhibits, and for maintaining only those animals the zoo could properly care for, and it was reflected in his emphasis on creating a strong education program.

It was during Finley’s tenure that the Potter Park Zoo Society would be profoundly reorganized, and the animal collection would be significantly improved. To accomplish this, Finley brought in two people who would reshape Potter Park Zoo through the rest of the century and beyond: animal curator Gerald Brady, who would later succeed Finley, and Zoo Society Director Carol Webster.

The redesigned logo for Potter Park Zoo Society (graphic courtesy Potter Park Zoo Society).

THE FRIENDS GET AN UPGRADE

After Ellen Lumbert resigned from the Friends of the Zoo, Jo Dickert, the wife of one of the zoo's keepers, Dave Dickert, took her place and would lead the Friends until 1989. This was a difficult time for many people. Potter Park Zoo was changing drastically and could no longer grow as much as it wanted to with the type of fund-raising efforts that characterized the Friends efforts up to that point. Zoos around the country were becoming more sophisticated, exhibits more pricey, and a new mission of education was coming into focus, which meant establishing education programs at the zoo.

Jo Dickert led the transition, along with another woman who was invited by Lansing City Councilwoman Alfreda Schmidt to be part of a new zoo board: Judi Corr. At the time, Corr was still a college student at Michigan State (she was returning to school as an adult after raising a family), where she was studying anthropology and conducted primate research with the organization EarthWatch, but she was actively involved in her community, including on the local opera board. Corr recalled her first steps into volunteering at the zoo:

> I called the Friends and attended a meeting, and that's where I met Jo Dickert.... Jo had, I think, a wider vision than many of the people did in that group. They were the hardest working, most directed people that cared about the zoo and that were doing things from the ground up. I mean, their penguin exhibit was amazing! But they had no idea where to go from there. They really didn't. And there comes a time, when you have organizations like that, that you have to bring different players in....
>
> I knew how, if you're going to change the community's attitude about things, you need to have the community, not only just the citizenship, but the corporate community involved. Because that's how you get the attention, and how you get the expertise. And Jo saw that, and she and I together were responsible for changing it.[6]

The Friends of the Zoo was renamed the Potter Park Zoological Society in 1986. The last years of the 1980s were a bumpy ride, as times of transition often are. According to Jo Dickert, between 1987 and 1989, there were actually two organizations: the Friends and the Society. Carol Webster, who took over from Mrs. Dickert in 1989, and Diane McNeil, the current Society director, assert on the contrary that there were never two organizations because the bylaws remained the same. Only the name changed from the Friends of the Zoo to the Potter Park Zoological Society. Corr explained that there was a definite changing of the guard, as she and Jo Dickert sought people with particular business skills to form the backbone of the new Society board:

> At that point, once we became—or started to become—the Zoological Society it was important to start bringing other people on board. You know, there were hard feelings.... [But] I think they [the Friends] recognized that, gee, if we're going to go any further this is what we need to do, and we don't know how to do it. So, Jo and I began to put people together to formulate the board. And we did it by going out into the community. Adam's Advertising, for instance, was brought on board. We got them to design the [new] logo, put up the billboard, do all that kind of stuff. And we brought in a person from Michigan Bell; we brought in a consultant or two.... We brought in quite a few [board members] from the surrounding community that were very involved. Not necessarily movers and shakers, and not necessarily what my grandmother would have called "moneyed people," but people with skills, and organization, and corporate support. I think we did pretty well with that.

A board of directors was organized to lead the Potter Park Zoological Society. Some of the volunteers who had been longtime Friends were asked to join the board, and some were not, which caused turmoil within the organization. Several devoted volunteers, such as the Lumberts, felt they were no longer appreciated, that they were being relegated to a kind of subcommittee that would be in charge of bake sales. Other members of the Friends resented the idea that the zoo was now going to seek big funding from such corporations as General Motors. They wanted the zoo to remain a largely family affair, with more modest objectives.

A controversial figure within all this mess was Tom Howes, who became a part-time president of the board of directors. Howes already had a full-time job working at a Flint hospital, and consequently did not devote much time to the zoo. Some would later accuse him of mismanaging Society money, spending funds irresponsibly for lunches and other entertainment.

Into the resulting chaos stepped two people who would be key to the Society's evolution: Carol Webster and Chris Ridings. Both had previously volunteered at zoos: Webster at the Buffalo and then Columbus Zoo, and Ridings at a zoo in Como, Minnesota. Together, they would be instrumental in establishing a core of docents (volunteer educators), and working with education director Kelliann Whitney to create various education programs for the zoo. Ridings, though she did a lot to help the zoo, did not remain there long. Webster, however, was to become a leader for many years to come.

CAROL WEBSTER COMES TO POTTER PARK ZOO

Carol Webster had been a volunteer at the Columbus Zoo, where she was also on the special events committee. She moved to Lansing when her husband, Frank, was hired to work for the National Education Association. She recalled:

> When I moved here, I did not want to come to Lansing. I was so in love with the Columbus Zoo. When I came in, our real estate agent said that the closest zoo was Binder Park in Battle Creek! And, when I moved here, we had been here about two and a half weeks … and a neighbor asked if I had ever been to Potter Park…. One thing led to another and that afternoon I went down to Potter Park Zoo. Boy, I'll tell you, my heart was in my hand! Here's a wonderful little park, right in the middle of downtown that nobody seemed to know about.
>
> I had trouble finding the entrance because the old entrance was kind of neglected back in the corner. Dave Dickert at that time was the senior keeper, and he was feeding one of the penguins by hand.

Zoo Society director Carol Webster helped modernize the organization and bring in big donors for the zoo (photo courtesy Potter Park Zoo Society).

> He looked up, and we just started to talk, and he said, "You seem to know a lot about zoos," and I was almost in tears. I told him the story that I was so happy to find the zoo.... At the time, his wife was president of the Zoological Society. Oddly enough, she called me that evening, and asked if I would have lunch with her and Doug Finley the following day.[7]

During that meeting, Jo Dickert and Finley talked with Webster about the upcoming reopening of the Feline/Primate Building. Webster inquired innocently whether a planned media event and official opening ceremony were planned. One hadn't been, and she found herself quickly put in charge of organizing it.

Beginning as a volunteer, Webster took the first docent class that was offered, graduating in 1986. The next year, she was hired by Finley to be the new Society director after Jo Dickert had stepped down. Unwittingly, she found herself the object of some scorn because people saw her as being associated with Doug Finley, who had rocked the boat so much at the zoo. "When I came on, there were some people who didn't even speak to me," she lamented. "And I didn't even know what the story was at that time." She would describe the loss of so many former Friends members as "a sin."

Eventually, though, relationships were patched up, and Webster became pals with the Lumberts and other former Friends, even those who had decided not to return to the zoo.

THE SOCIETY MISSION

Recovering from what was an admittedly ugly transitional period, Webster got down to work. The Friends had done all they could have to keep the Potter Park Zoo alive through the 1970s and 1980s, but now the zoo needed more. For example, there was still a problem with staffing, with many workers only being part-time, including Rick Parker, who was in charge of concessions, Judy Kish, who was office manager, and the Society director. Webster found the money to make Parker and Kish full-time employees so that they would have the time to do their jobs right. Next, she set about leading a beautification project, including getting new flower gardens planted, painting buildings, and upgrading the gift shop, which at the time was located in the former train station.

"The gift shop had ... birds flying around inside it; it was one big room. It was a rubber snake shop," as Webster described it. Improving the gift shop would do much to raise needed revenues. She found people "who had never been asked before" to help with the gift shop, providing labor and materials. "There has always been a ton of people who really cared, and that's how it happened." She added, "We did lots and lots of things. I was just sitting there. It's everybody else that did it. People love the zoo."

Like a little dynamo in the midst of the zoo, Webster was to the new Society what Jim Hough had been to the Friends. She might not take credit for it, rightly saying that many others did much of the work, but without her leadership the Society would not have coalesced into the goal-oriented, mission-driven nonprofit organization it is today.

Webster took a three-pronged approach to aiding the zoo through her Society office: 1) Find a base of private and corporate donors; 2) establish a strong volunteer and education program; and 3) reacquaint the community to the zoo.

Raising money, of course, was always key. The funds from the bond issue had been spent, and its five-year term was over. Doug Finley successfully rallied to have a 0.71 millage passed in 1989, which raised $1.4 million a year. Voters, who saw their zoo improve dramatically when the Feline/Primate House opened in May 1989 at

Carol Webster accepts a $500,000 donation from the Hal and Jean Glassen Memorial Foundation in 2004. The foundation later donated the funds for the new river otter exhibit. Bringing in big donors such as this has been key to many of the zoo's improvements (photo courtesy Potter Park Zoo Society).

a final cost of about $2.4 million (up $900,000 from the original budget!), were inspired to do more. The ballot initiative easily passed. Initially, most of this money went to the zoo, but over the years—especially in the years since the new millennium—more and more of it has been siphoned off by city government for other projects. The money had originally been intended for capital improvements, but in recent years it has been used increasingly simply to pay for operational expenses.

The money from the bonds would not start coming in until 1990, however, and Webster vowed that the Society could do even more by raising $5 million in private donations. This money would go to several new projects, including a modern concession stand near the Feline/Primate House, improvements to the Barnyard and Petting Zoo, which were completed in 1992, laying down fresh walkways, and a brand-new pony trail next to the Barnyard that replaced the old carousel.

Part of Webster's strategy for raising money was to initiate a Society Membership program. Previously, volunteers of the Friends and the Society only were "members" of the zoo, but Webster wanted to bring in the general public. So, for a modest annual fee, anyone could be a Society Member and receive benefits, such as free annual admission to the zoo, without having to be a volunteer (this was after the admission fee was implemented). She also made the rounds to area banks, law firms, and other potential donors, such as those at the Walnut Hills Country Club, where her husband was a member. Webster was not too proud to ask anyone and everyone she came across to help the zoo: "I don't care if somebody says 'No' to me, because if you go to enough places you'll get some yeses."

There were many more ideas to come besides selling memberships, too. For example, Webster initiated the Adopt an Animal program in 1989. For a fee ranging from $10 and upwards of $100 or even $500, depending on the animal, anyone could call him- or herself an adoptive parent of a Potter Park Zoo animal. The money that came in went to improve exhibits. For example, $5,500 was used in 1990 to make updates to the grey wolf exhibit.

Finally, the new Society director revamped and added to the special events at the zoo. For example, what had once been the Christmas Open House that lasted a day during winter reemerged in 1993 as the Wonderland of Lights, a spectacle of holiday decorations, choir and ensemble music, and special activities that now runs from late-November through the New Year. The Halloween event the Friends had organized was expanded in the somewhat more elaborate Boo at the Zoo, and many more activities were planned throughout the year. These now include such innovative festivities as International Migratory Bird Day and L&L Food Days (originally Goff Days, before L&L bought out that grocery store chain), the latter a collaboration with a local grocery chain.

Webster summarized her strategy for raising awareness about the zoo this way: "It was three steps: It was education—getting to the children and the schools and having them get fired up about bringing their families to the zoo; then, Wonderland of Lights and going to the mayors in all the communities and inviting them to buy into this great activity that their constituents loved already; and the third thing … was when Gerry Brady was able to bring in some 'hot' animals. When we were able to bring in the tigers and when we were able to get the rhinos. We were the smallest zoo in the country to have black rhinos from the SSP…. Gerry was able to wheel and deal, and animals are what the zoo is all about. He was able to bring in some animals that we could say, 'Here's your little zoo, and it's still a really important part of conservation.'"

One of the most successful annual events at Potter Park Zoo is the holiday season Wonderland of Lights (photo courtesy Mary Anne McNamara).

Zoo director Gerry Brady (left) poses with wildlife conservationist and television personality Jack Hanna (photo courtesy Potter Park Zoo).

GERRY BRADY BRINGS ANIMAL CONSERVATION FOCUS TO POTTER PARK

Gerry Brady, who is currently the director of Potter Park Zoo, was hired in 1989 by a committee (led by Doug Finley) to be the zoo's general curator. Brady at the time was already general curator at the Cheyenne Mountain Zoo in Colorado Springs, Colorado, so stepping in to this role at Lansing's zoo was not a complicated transition. But Finley also brought him in specifically because of Brady's connections with the AZA's SSP program going back fifteen years.

"When I first got here the animal collection was terrible," as Brady described it in his opinion. "They had raccoons in one of the exhibits in the small moats, and they had bears and coyotes on the back side of the Bird House. There was one elephant here. Immediately, I tried to get to know all the keepers and tried to get to know the exhibits and the animals.... The first thing I did was I got rid of the raccoons, and replaced those with bears."[8] The large moats by the Bird House were described by Brady as awful conditions for animals—just as Finley had said—and they were quickly closed; the coyotes that were there were sent to a nature center. Brady set up an agreement with Bear Country in South Dakota to bring in bear cubs each year to Potter Park. Each year in the fall, when the cubs had started to get too large, they were returned to South Dakota. The cubs proved a popular attraction for about a decade at the zoo until the AZA recommended discontinuing the arrangement because of questionable management of the animals at Bear Country.[9]

Wildlife in Zoos: The Continuing Debate

Although I have already touched on this issue, it is worth discussing again at this point. The debate about animals in zoos is certainly not limited to large pachyderms. There are many animal rights groups throughout the world that do not believe that animals belong in zoos at all. Among the most vocal of these is PETA (People for the Ethical Treatment of Animals), whose members are actually against animal ownership of any kind, even when it comes to cats and dogs as companion animals. Others are less extreme than PETA, but no less vehement in their opposition to zoos. In his *Inhumane Society,* for example, author Michael W. Fox expressed his opinion that it would be better to allow species to go extinct than to keep them confined in zoos.[10]

A lot of opposition to zoos comes from the fact that they force wild animals to live in confined spaces and depend on humans for food and other necessities. This is, unfortunately, very true. Zoo supporters, of course, would counter that zoos stem species extinctions while educating people about the importance of wildlife.

Another rather famous opponent of zoos is Alan Green, whose *Animal Underground* is a diatribe against how zoos breed and trade animals.[11] Green opines that too often zoos breed animals with the purpose of attracting visitors, rather than just preserving species. The result is that sometimes there is a surplus of unwanted animals. These animals are traded through announcements in the AZA's *Animal Exchange* newsletter. The problem then begins when disreputable dealers pick up these available animals and, through a series of convoluted acts made to cover their tracks with forged, lost, or misleading documentation, transport them to roadside zoos, private owners, or to those who use them for "canned shoots." In the latter case, endangered animals are placed in fenced-in areas and, for a fee, a "hunter" can very easily shoot them for trophies. (I think it is significant to note here that Green nowhere mentions Potter Park Zoo in his book, though several other zoos are discussed.)

The black bear cubs were always cute and playful, making them hugely popular with zoo guests (photo courtesy Mary Anne McNamara).

I once interviewed Detroit Zoo director Ron Kagan for another book about animal welfare. He pointed out, quite astutely, that zoos are not the problem; it is the few people who would abuse animals who are the problem. The majority of those who work at zoos are doing everything they possibly can to help the wild creatures in their care, but every now and then you will find a bad egg rotting in the nest. True, zoos were, once upon a time, places using animals for the benefit of people. There has been a huge change since then. Today, zoos are here to protect animals and to inspire human beings to join in their crusade.

Brady also teamed with Finley to move Tombi to a better facility as well. "It was just unacceptable to have an elephant by itself, and we couldn't afford to get another one because we'd have to spend a few million dollars making all those improvements."

It was a major coup for Potter Park Zoo when Brady then arranged for black rhinoceroses to be exhibited in Lansing. Other interesting species soon followed, including meerkats from Africa, binturongs (also known as bearcats) from Southeast Asia, Rocky Mountain bighorn sheep, bongos, red pandas, snow leopards, and Bali mynah birds. Although the zoo had had tigers before, Brady, who was in

An endangered snow leopard. Potter Park Zoo has had great success breeding this rare Asian feline (photo by Bruce Bolender courtesy of the Potter Park Zoo Society).

The former Monkey Island has been converted into an exhibit for Rocky Mountain Bighorn Sheep. This was easy to do as the rocky exhibit mimics this species' habitat perfectly (photo by Bruce Bolender courtesy of the Potter Park Zoo Society).

charge of the Sumatran tiger SSP, described it as a "terrible program." What he meant was that they were tigers who were not considered good animals for breeding purposes to keep the endangered species population healthy. So, Brady made arrangements with the AZA for SSP tigers. Although he was specially knowledgeable about Sumatran tigers, he obtained Siberian (also known as Amur) tigers because they acclimated better to Michigan's colder climate.

The logic behind all these efforts was to transform Potter Park Zoo from a zoological garden whose animals were brought in mainly for visitor appeal and turn it into a vital participant in the AZA community that played a major role in the conservation of endangered species. As with Doug Finley, sometimes Brady's insistent and goal-oriented approach rubbed staff members the wrong way. However, within a few years he had obtained a large population of rare and endangered species at Potter Park, the likes of which had never before been seen in the past seventy years of the zoo's existence.

Adorable red pandas are an important addition to the zoo's SSP program (photo by Bruce Bolender courtesy of the Potter Park Zoo Society).

"My main goal as curator was to provide more training for the keepers," Brady summarized, "to improve nutrition, to get the exhibits changed so they were more aesthetic, more appealing to the public, better for the animals, to change the entire animal collection so there was education and conservation goals, and that's what I've been doing."

When Doug Finley stepped down as zoo director, Brady was promoted to take his place while concurrently holding the post of general curator. The dual job of managing budgetary and staffing issues, along with the importance of animal care, was an onerous one that has more recently been relieved by the hiring of Dr. Tara Harrison in 2003, the zoo veterinarian who now is also the head curator.

No More Free Zoo

Zoo attendance, which had dropped somewhat with the addition of the parking fee, started to rise again by the late 1980s. Between 1985

Scimitar-horned oryx graze at the zoo. These animals became extinct in the wild, and so it was a thrill when a baby was born at the zoo in 2007 (photo by Constance Wardell courtesy of Potter Park Zoo Society).

Meerkats from South Africa have a lot of personality. The media can often play a role in a species' popularity. For example, the Animal Planet television series *Meerkat Manor* and the Disney film *The Lion King* have made meerkats familiar to many children. Seeing the actual animal can be quite an eye-opening, educational experience (photo by Bruce Bolender courtesy of the Potter Park Zoo Society).

and 1988, it inched up by a few thousand guests a year, but when the Feline/Primate House renovation was completed in 1989, it shot up from 318,071 in 1988 to 380,862 the next year. Encouraged by their success, and with so many changes to the Society and zoo leadership, it was as if Potter Park Zoo was being reborn a second time. If the first renaissance had been in 1969, then the second was surely marked by the year 1989.

Amidst all the excitement, however, the budget issue raised its ugly, hoary head yet again. It was an issue that always plagued Lansing's zoo. In 1990, Mayor Terry McKane said that operations should be turned over completely to the Zoological Society, relieving the city of the burden of keeping the zoo in the parks department budget. The notion was one that would be proposed off and on again over the next fifteen years, but it was completely unfeasible in 1990. While the Society was no doubt doing a good job, it was in a supportive role only. There was no way Webster and her staff could pay for salaries, benefits, building maintenance, utilities, taxes, animal care and more. Even if it managed to do so, it would mean the end of any improvements because there would be no money left after the essentials were paid for.

Some pointed out that John Ball Zoo in Grand Rapids and Binder Park Zoo in Battle Creek were both run by zoo societies, but the situations there were not comparable, Webster explained. For one thing, the transition at John Ball had been accomplished over several years; for another, Binder Park was the lucky recipient of monies from the wealthy and generous Kellogg Foundation; John Ball Zoo is also located in a city where it has been able to find large corporate sponsors, such as Steel Case, Amway, and the grocery chain Meijer, Inc. Regionalization was another thought, which involved having one or more counties support the zoo financially, but Webster felt it wasn't the time for that either.

To stave off such drastic changes, it was decided instead to implement an admission fee for the zoo. The fee was negligible: just $1.50 for adults and fifty cents for children five to fourteen years of age, with younger children being free. Furthermore, the fee would only apply to non-Lansing residents.

Though Potter Park Zoo had been one of the last zoological parks in the United States to create an admissions fee (only 12 of the 157 zoos in the country accredited by the AZA were still completely free in 1991), many people were in an uproar over the decision. In one *Lansing State Journal* editorial, journalist Sheila Schimpf went so far as to assert that it would sound the death knell for the zoo, and even the city itself. "As the zoo goes, so goes the city,"[12] Schimpf asserted, predicting that visitors from outside the city would feel alienated by an admission fee, and adding that those in the suburbs would likely go to malls instead. Berating the City Council, Schimpf concluded: "When they made a distinction between those who pay property taxes and those who pay income taxes, council members lost more than they bargained for."

Of course, in retrospect, it's easy to see that Schimpf was completely off base. The zoo's attendance continued to be strong, with over sixty percent of visitors arriving from outside Lansing.

GOOD-BYE, ELVIS, SAY "HELLO" TO CARL FOR US

Amongst all these significant changes in the late 1980s and early 1990s at the zoo, one more needs to be addressed. The final severing of ties between Potter Park Zoo and the Fenner Nature Center came in 1980, when the center was placed under its own administration separate from the zoo. However, there were still some ties between the two organizations while there were animals being cared for by zoo staff at the Mt. Hope facility. According to Dr. Jim Sikarskie, the U.S. Department of Agriculture was not even aware that Potter Park Zoo and the Fenner Nature Center had had an ongoing management relationship for decades, so when this tie was finally unknotted, it went unnoticed by many. The man who founded the center, Carl Fenner, had passed away in 1991, but it was not until the last animal managed by the zoo, Elvis the Bison, died in 2003 that the zoo finally cut its association off completely.

Elvis's death was foreshadowed years earlier by the continuing decline in the animal collection at the nature center; its focus had become more aimed at education and on the animals that visited the Fenner grounds naturally, because they were endemic to the area. In 1993, the very popular Sam the Eagle, who had been a beloved attraction there for three decades, died, much to the grief of the local community. The bison herd, which had once been rather numerous at Fenner, was whittled down, animal by animal, until Elvis alone remained by 1995. Dr. Sikarskie and the folks at Potter Park wanted to move Elvis to a sanctuary where he could be with others of his own kind. Bison, being social animals, prefer to live in herds rather than fending for themselves alone.

However, the neighboring community by the Fenner Nature Center had grown so attached to Elvis that they put strong political pressure on city government to keep the bison where he was. Dolores Maidlow-Kramer, who at the time was acting president of the Forest View Citizens Association, expressed her outrage at the plan, asserting that local citizens had wanted to bring more bison in to keep Elvis company years ago, but that the Parks and Recreation director had refused, saying that animals do not get lonely. Then, in 1995, the director changed his position, acknowledging that the animal did indeed get lonely and had to be moved. His motivation, according to Maidlow-Kramer, was to do whatever was needed for financial reasons. The initial motivation of denying bison purchases had been to save money; the new motivation to get rid of Elvis had been so that the ten acres of land occupied by the bison at Fenner could be sold for a profit, Maidlow-Kramer pointed out.[13]

Eventually, with additional support from City Council member Sandy Allen, Elvis was allowed to remain at Fenner. "We had to spend a ton of money retrofitting the exhibit over there,"[14] recalled Dr. Sikarskie, because the fencing had been deemed inadequate when the USDA finally got wind of the fact that bison were kept there in close contact with people. According to keeper Jan Brigham, even if Elvis had been moved to a sanctuary, he would have had to be placed in a bachelor herd. "I had contacted the wildlife biologist at Yellowstone, who specializes in bison, and she told me that we could never put cows back in with him, because he would probably kill them because he'd been by himself. [The biologist] thought a bachelor group would have worked, and that's what we were trying to do at that time."[15] Elvis spent the next eight years of his life alone, until severe arthritis became so painful for him that he could not stand up. He was humanely euthanized by Dr. Sikarskie in 2003.

With the last bison finally gone, the Arboretum—now the Fenner Nature Center—could go on its own independent path, which includes the important mission of educating people in the wonders of native Michigan plants and animals, while the Potter Park Zoo could focus its renewed efforts on animal conservation and taking care of its new exotic and highly endangered species.

RHINOS: THE NEW PACHYDERM

Probably one of the most symbolic animals at Potter Park Zoo to represent the park's dramatic change in its collection and philosophy

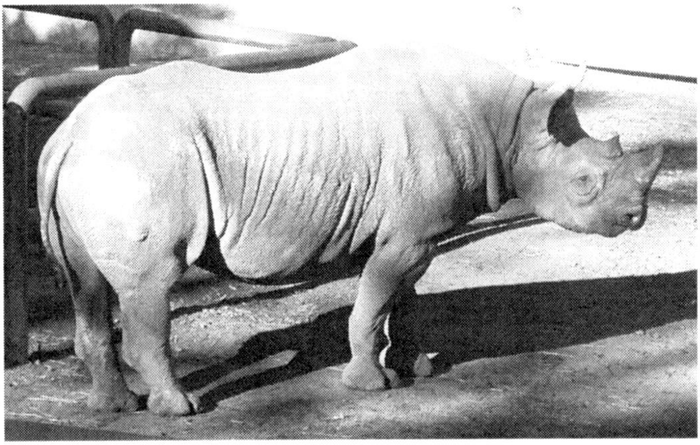

White rhinos became the new big pachyderm at Potter Park Zoo after Tombi left (photo by Constance Wardell courtesy of Potter Park Zoo Society).

are the black rhinos. While it had been resolved that the zoo did not have the necessary facilities to maintain either Bingo or Tombi, black rhinoceroses were a completely different matter. Unlike their African cousins, white rhinos, black rhinos are more solitary creatures and perfectly content to be by themselves.

However, it was not Gerry Brady's plan to have just one rhino at Potter Park. He intended to bring in a female and male in the SSP program as a breeding pair, thus making Lansing's zoo the smallest in the country to participate in a black rhino breeding program. The zoo renovated the former elephant house at a cost of $110,000 to ready it for the needs of the new, special megavertebrate to reside at the zoo.

Mashaki was the name of the first black rhino to arrive in Lansing. Weighing in at 1,500 pounds, the three-year-old Mashaki was imported from the San Diego Zoo in 1990. As a young rhino, he had a reputation for being a bit of a troublemaker, which is how he got his Swahili name, which means "trouble." A popular new animal for the zoo, Mashaki was well known for his love of apples, and in just the short expanse of three years he gained 2,500 pounds to weigh in at two full tons. He must have eaten a lot of apples!

In 1994, however, Mashaki was moved to the San Francisco Zoo to be paired up with a female named Elly. This is one of the potential hazards of participating in an SSP program, because if it is determined by the AZA that a certain animal should be moved elsewhere in order to breed, then the zoo maintaining that animal needs to comply for the sake of the species.

In those three years, Brady had established that his zoo could keep a black rhino healthy and happy, and so Mashaki was replaced in 1994 by a male named Jimma and a female named Ebony. This was the name by which she was known by the keepers, though she also had a public name: Rafiki, which means "friend" in Swahili. This came about when Brady held a name-the-rhino contest as a promotion for the zoo. The winner was a two-and-a-half-year-old boy from Okemos named DeShawn Trune, who, with the help of his mother, came up with the name.

Rhino Lips

There are currently five species of rhinoceros in the world: the white and black rhinos from Africa that are familiar to most Americans, and the more rare Indian, Javan, and Sumatran varieties. The Sumatran, though the smallest of the five, is particularly striking in that it grows shaggy reddish hair. White rhinos are the largest and can weigh up to 4,000 pounds, while black rhinos are slightly smaller at 3,000 pounds, but still impressive. Of the African varieties, the white is more common, while poaching has reduced black rhino numbers in the wild to approximately 3,000 (about twenty-five percent of the 1968 population).

The easiest way to tell the African species apart, aside from size, is by the lip and mouth shape. White rhinos have a wide mouths designed for grazing grasses, while blacks have narrower mouths with a triangular-shaped, prehensile lip adapted for plucking leaves off shrubs. The names do not refer to these rhinos' coloration; rather the white rhino got its name from its lip. Dutch settlers in South Africa named them "weit," which means "wide," and this was later turned into "white" by the English. After that, it just seemed natural to distinguish Africa's other rhino by calling it "black."

As a docent, one of my most memorable experiences was hand-feeding a black rhino. Standing next to this huge, muscular creature, I handed it little food pellets, which it gingerly grasped with its sensitive prehensile lip. Rhinos have been known to charge people and can be dangerous, but these herbivorous browsers can be remarkably placid and gentle, as well.

A great deal had, indeed, changed at Potter Park Zoo by the early 1990s. Though it had been difficult, even painful, at times to see its way toward becoming the type of facility that is now considered a modern-day zoo, the zoo staff and Society could honestly say that they had made the transition successfully. Years of struggle simply to

Mashaki gets a specially-made rhino cake treat before leaving the zoo (photo courtesy Potter Park Zoo).

maintain a zoo with interesting animals that were well cared for had at last been rewarded. Potter Park Zoo could begin to establish and expand upon the missions of conservation, education, research, and, of course, recreation and enjoyment for all its visitors.

7

Zoo Keepers and Animal Care

So far, the attention has been on the many challenges faced by the staff and its supporters just to keep Potter Park Zoo afloat and improve it wherever possible. Much of the work in changing the zoo has been due to the work of the Zoo Society, and, of course, zoo supervisors such as Ted Downey, Jerry Miller, Doug Finley, and Gerry Brady.

But while all the fund raising, master planning, political arguing, and philosophical debates lingered on through the decades, someone has been behind the scenes the whole time doing the daily work that is vital and central to all zoos: taking care of the animals. These people, of course, are the zoo keepers and veterinarians who keep the animals alive, healthy, and, hopefully, happy.

Everyday visitors coming to Potter Park Zoo—or any other zoo for that matter—often see zoo keepers on the grounds feeding the animals, raking the enclosures, or doing less glamorous jobs, like the unenviable poop scooping. Other times, guests may see keepers simply observing the animals. Except for picking up after the inevitable messes animals leave in their exhibits, it may seem to many outsiders, especially those who are animal lovers, like the ideal job: plenty of outdoor activities, working with fascinating species that most people never see, and doing one's part in the conservation mission.

That, as they say, is only the tip of the iceberg.

"There's much more to the job than raking up every day," explained one very experienced Potter Park zoo keeper, Mary Anne McNamara (an employee from 1977 to 2002). "Something that we all have to deal with is people's misconception [that] working the zoo is so cool and it would be so much fun. I'm not saying that either one of those is incorrect, but there's got to be an interpretation of those two words. For a person who always wanted to be a zoo keeper those two words certainly apply. However, the person who is not in the profession very often has a misconception about what a keeper actually does. [Visitors] might see a summer employee who is not cleaning at the time. They don't understand that all the cleaning [may have] happened before the area opens to the public for the day. And maybe the keeper is standing in the goat yard doing what appears to be nothing, and an animal may come up to them and lean against their leg. The keeper—the summer keeper—reaches down and scratches their ears or whatever. And there are a lot of people who think that that is what zookeeping is."[1]

Zookeeping is definitely *not* about "playing with the animals all day," said McNamara, and any other keeper would surely agree. Human holidays and weekends are meaningless to animals. When Christmas rolls around, or a sunny, pleasant weekend when many of us would rather be playing golf or traveling, animals at the zoo still need to be fed, their exhibits cleaned, and their health watched over.

As with many zoos around the country, keepers at Potter Park are usually assigned to certain areas of the zoo. This helps them become very familiar with certain animals so that they can recognize any signs of distress in them early (keepers are the first line of defense when it comes to spotting a sick animal), but they also rotate responsibilities on occasion so that *all* the keepers are at least acquainted with every animal in the park and understand their special, individual needs. This way, if a keeper has to take a day off to rest or because he or she is ill, or if a keeper retires, there is always someone there who can fill in.

Zoo keepers at Potter Park are organized into four main groups: the Rhino Crew (formerly known as the Doghouse Crew because their area centered on the old building that used to house canine species), the Birdhouse Crew (centered on the Bird/Reptile House), the Feline/Primate House Crew, and the Penguin Crew. The keepers in these crews cover more animals than just those indicated by the crew names. For example, the Rhino Crew generally takes care of other

Keepers Janice Tomlian and Sarah Foote enjoy working in the Rhino Crew. Despite the name, these keepers are responsible for helping in the care of all the animals throughout the zoo (photo courtesy Potter Park Zoo).

hoof stock animals, such as big horn sheep and camels; the Penguin crew is a kind of floating crew that handles the species not covered by the other keepers, such as ostriches, oryx, and wolves. Up until early 2007, Potter Park Zoo had eleven keepers. Eight keepers were organized into pairs of two for each of the four crews, while the remaining three keepers were floaters who worked in every area of the zoo, helping out in a rotation wherever they were needed. This number increased to fourteen by 2008.

THE EVOLUTION OF THE KEEPER

Just as Potter Park Zoo has evolved considerably over the decades, so has the job of zoo keeper. Back in the early days, when animal care was not thought of as a very scientific job, keepers were hired by the City of Lansing and usually transferred from other positions in the Parks and Recreation Department. Bill Swix, for example, was hired into the Parks department as a maintenance man, and was working as head of maintenance at Fenner Arboretum when he was moved to his keeper position in 1960. At the time, people really knew very little about taking care of wild animals, so there was not a big emphasis on scientific training as a requirement for employment.

Keeper Lisle Scutt handles a woolly monkey in this undated photo, c. 1960s. The philosophy of animal management has changed greatly since then, with keepers taking an increasingly hands-off approach in order to keep animals as wild as possible (photo courtesy Maisie Downey).

Today, however, that has changed dramatically. Generally, the zoo seeks employees who have at least some college education in a field related to zoology or biology, with two- or four-year degrees preferred. They are also required to pass a written test before they are considered for a position. Fortunately for the Lansing zoo, it is located very close to one of the finest universities in the country in the area of zoo and veterinary sciences: Michigan State University in East Lansing. Also, as Director Gerry Brady pointed out, the City has actually been very generous when it comes to paying its keepers, who are all union members (United Auto Workers 2256). Because Potter Park pays well, the zoo is able to attract quality graduates from MSU. Brady mentioned, for instance, that Binder Park Zoo in Battle Creek is privately owned and therefore pays its new keepers comparatively little. They often hire high school graduates and then train them on the job to be keepers. "The AZA does not mandate that we have to hire [college] graduates," noted Brady. "We are just lucky to be in the position that we're able to hire people that have a college education in zoo and aquarium science.... When they come in they're smart, they're hard working, and then they get trained to care for rhinos and tigers, and that gets you your experienced staff."[2]

According to an issue of *Occupational Outlook Quarterly,* animal caretakers earn an average of $17,120 annually, as of 2001.[3] This, then, is obviously not one of the more high-paying jobs one can find, but the rewards for animal lovers who wish to work in the field are numerous, which is why one finds zoo keepers to be such dedicated employees.

"Keepers in general," asserted McNamara, "... stay in that profession.... Some people move from one zoo to another. They usually do that when they're single.... But the keepers at Potter Park for years tended to be married, so they basically stayed in the community." There has consequently been very little turnover at the zoo, with openings only coming along generally when someone retires.

Keepers also regularly take classes and attend seminars outside of the zoo to keep their knowledge up to date. Thanks to support from the Friends in the 1970s, funding was provided to start sending keepers to such classes, which had not been done previously due to lack of funds. Today, that kind of extra education is essential in the increasingly complex field of animal care.

Zoo keepers are managed by animal curators. At larger zoos, such as the Detroit Zoo, there will often be several curators who specialize in different types of animals. For example, a large zoo could have a curator of mammals, a curator of birds, a curator of marine animals, and a curator of herpetology (reptiles and amphibians). Potter Park Zoo is far too small for such luxuries, so all this responsibility falls under Dr. Tara Myers Harrison's charge, along with support from Gerry Brady.

FEEDING AND CLEANING

One of the highlights of a visit to any zoo is when guests have a chance to see the animals being fed by the keepers. For many species, especially those with more nocturnal tendencies, this is their most active time, and it's fun to watch them. For the keepers, feedings are the most time-consuming part of their jobs, and one of the most important. Food has to be carefully prepared to make certain that diets are well balanced, and vegetables and meats must be as fresh as possible (no canned and few frozen foods, which lose much of their nutrients). In some cases, vitamin and medicine supplements are added to maintain animal health. For example, the Magellanic penguins at Potter Park are fed frozen fish. Because their food is frozen,

Keeper Dennis Sweeney feeds the penguins frozen capelins. Keeping track of what animals eat and how much is extremely important because the first sign that an animal is sick may be indicated by a change in its appetite (photo by Bruce Bolender courtesy of the Potter Park Zoo Society).

vitamins are lost; therefore, extra vitamins have to be put into the fish. In addition, because filling their pool with saltwater would be expensive, and it also rusts plumbing, the penguin pool contains fresh water. Penguins are saltwater birds, however, and they have special glands near their beaks that allow them to strain out salt from ocean waters they have drunk. At zoos, with only freshwater to drink and swim in, these glands can atrophy from lack of use. The penguins therefore receive sea tabs to provide them with the salt they need to stay healthy. Furthermore, penguins are vulnerable to avian malaria, so they receive a dose of the drugs Sulfadiazine and Pyremethamine to decrease the chances of infection from the malaria parasite. Since penguins swallow their food whole, administering such pills is simple: keepers place them inside fish gills, then feed the fish to the penguins—too bad cats aren't as cooperative!

Keepers maintain careful records of what each animal eats. This is because the first sign of an animal being unwell is when it starts to refuse food. Many animals are notorious for hiding the fact that they are sick, primarily because sickness would make them an easy target for predators or rivals of their own species. By the time most people notice an animal is not feeling well, whatever is causing the problem—whether it is a disease or injury—may have progressed too far to save the animal in time.

Identifying Animals

Even though keepers at Potter Park Zoo become very familiar with the animals under their care, sometimes it can be difficult to tell some of them apart, such as the penguins or the Patagonian hares. Sometimes, this can be done when animals have distinctive colorations, such as stripes on tigers or bongos; photographs may be used, too, to keep a record of distinguishing marks.

When appearance alone is not enough, the keepers use other means to tell animals apart, including:

- Microchips
- Tattoos
- Ear notches (used for pigs)
- Ear or neck tags (often used for hoof stock, ostriches, kangaroos, and wallabies)
- Leg or wing bands (used for birds)
- Necklaces or collars (e.g., used on lemurs)

Some animals at the zoo, such as the lions and tigers, are easy to keep track of in terms of dietary consumption. Others, such as the penguins and ring-tailed lemurs, are much more problematic, because they look very similar to human eyes. Therefore, to keep records of their health more easily, such animals are given some form of identification. For example, the lemurs wear color-coded necklaccs, the penguins have I.D.'s on their wings, and the ostriches have tags put in their necks similar to ear piercings. Keepers then note the identification on each animal as they either feed them manually (as with the penguins) or watch as they eat in a more general free-for-all (as with lemurs or the spider monkeys) where food is spread throughout the enclosure .

In addition to food, cleanliness is also essential. A domestic cat may easily be trained to a litter box—or, as some people have done, even a toilet!—but wild animals have no such scruples. In their natural habitat, this is no problem, since they have wide open spaces to roam about in. At a zoo, where space is limited, droppings and urine can accumulate quickly. Daily cleaning, seven days a week, twelve months a year, all year long, is not a luxury that can be neglected. Filthy quarters foster infections and create breeding grounds for dis-

Keeper Dave Dickert watches over the tapirs in this c. 1970s photo (photo courtesy Potter Park Zoo).

One of the thrills of being a zoo keeper is taking care of the little ones, such as these wolf cubs, which are obviously a delight to keepers Mary Gandy and Walt Marcus (photo courtesy Potter Park Zoo).

ease. This problem is multiplied by the fact that zoos in more recent decades have tried to make enclosures more natural-looking. In the past, when animals such as bears, elephants, and lions were commonly held in concrete cages surrounded by iron bars, cleaning an exhibit was as simple as spraying it down with a hose and some disinfectant. Today, scooping the poop and removing urine is much more time-intensive. It isn't a pleasant job, but somebody's got to do it.

The American Association of Zoo Keepers, Inc.

Founded in 1967 in San Diego, California, the American Association of Zoo Keepers, Inc. (AAZK) is an organization of about 2,800 keepers, curators, veterinarians, vet techs, students, animal health technicians, and volunteers at zoos and aquariums. Through conferences, journals such as *Animal Keepers' Forum,* the dissemination of reports, studies, and other literature, and other means of communication, the AAZK encourages the education of its members so that they are as informed as possible of current animal care techniques. Although the name of this organization refers to this country, the AAZK has members from twenty-four foreign countries, as well.

The very existence of the AAZK demonstrates how the philosophy of zoo and aquarium animal care has evolved since the 1960s. Before then, keepers may have been looked upon as glorified pooper scoopers (and even today, many people think that a keeper's only job is feeding and cleaning up after the animals), but today there is a considerable degree of professionalism within this profession.

The AAZK not only serves as a resource for educating its members, but it also emphasizes the importance of educating the public about wildlife conservation.

THE UNEXPECTED SIDE OF ZOOKEEPING

Because the keepers at Potter Park Zoo are unionized, they are not allowed to work overtime without approval should they get behind in their day-to-day duties. Once 4:30 p.m. rolls around, the keepers are supposed to finish up and be gone for the day. This makes the feeding and cleaning process a bit more stressful because *all* the animals must be fed and *all* the animals must be cleaned up after without delay. Normally, when nothing unusual has happened, the work can run smoothly. When a keeper becomes ill and has to take a few days off, this can prove to be an inconvenience, but is usually handled by the flexible staff. Much more irksome are those unexpected surprises one inevitably runs across when wild animals and people mix.

Before security was beefed up at Potter Park Zoo, keepers ended up doing much of that work themselves—and they still keep their wary eyes open for potential problems. At one point, according to keeper Jan Brigham, who has been at Lansing zoo since 1975, the zoo tried to install a motion-detector security system that used light beams. "We started having trouble, though," Brigham recalled. "We had chickens and [they] … would set the alarm off."[4] Roaming peafowl did not help, either, so the system had to be abandoned.

Sometimes tragedy results not so much through deliberate abuse of animals, but through the public's ignorance or carelessness. One flagrant example of this occurred in early 2006, when a zoo visitor dropped a small rubber football next to the fishing cat's enclosure, or perhaps they pushed the ball through the enclosure fence. The ball was left there, and, apparently during the night sometime, the fishing cat was able to draw the ball into its cage, chew on it, and swallow many pieces of it. These pieces lodged in its stomach and ultimately resulted in its death despite the efforts of the zoo vet. The shame of it all was amplified by the fact that this particular animal—an increasingly rare species from Southeast Asia—was a young breeding cat that was valuable for the SSP program, and plans were being made to transfer it to another zoo for breeding.

Not that guests and projectiles are anything new. For example, in 1950 picnickers threw dry ice at some young bears and an ocelot at Potter Park. The animals ate the ice and perished. In another incident in the 1960s, Maisie Downey, wife of then-zoo manager Ted Downey, found a man throwing cigarette butts at Adam the chimp because he thought the chimp's reaction was "funny." Mrs. Downey grabbed his arm and led him to her husband, who no doubt read him the riot act.

Another instance of public neglect involves stray pets. Some people let their cats, for example, roam freely. Being small animals, domestic cats can easily wander into the zoo, where they spread potentially lethal diseases to the zoo's residents. In June 2006, two stray dogs dug under a fence and killed three Patagonian hares and injured a fourth. Thanks to the spirit of international zoo cooperation that exists today, the Toronto Zoo in Canada heard about Potter Park's loss and generously donated five of their own Patagonian hares to the Lansing zoo.

Some human escapades can be a little more humorous, or even bizarre. Back in 1978, one memorable zoo visitor, who is still recalled by many of the keepers who were there at the time as the "Naked Man in the Bird House," was obviously high on drugs when he was first spotted by now-retired keeper Walt Marcus. Marcus is remembered fondly for his soft Southern accent and utterly unflappable personality. When he found the man, buck naked, in the Bird House, Marcus famously made the to-the-point observation without blinking: "Boy, you better put some clothes on." "I don't think anything ever shocked him," noted Brigham wryly.

Instead of taking this sage advice, the man sprinted out of the Bird House. "He decided he wanted to ride our bull elk." Brigham related, "which fortunately was a younger one. He kicked the gate down and went in and just started yelling at the animal, 'I'm going to ride you!' Then he said, 'Go ahead, call the police, I don't care.'" The police, of course, were called and hauled him away. "They never did find out who he was or what was going on with him for sure."

Marcus's equanimity in atypical situations was tested again when he found a man and a woman under a blanket on zoo grounds. They were naked and going at it like bunnies on an unsubtle nature program. Marcus calmly told them they shouldn't be doing that at the zoo and got them to put their clothes on and leave.

The "Naked Man in the Bird House" certainly could have been injured severely for riding the elk, but other incidents of misbehavior have been even scarier. For instance, one time Mary Anne McNamara witnessed a zoo patron sticking her arms through the bars at the African leopard exhibit. Rushing over to the leopards with another keeper in tow, she yanked the woman away from the fence and asked her what the heck she thought she was trying to do. The woman explained she wanted to take a picture without any bars in the way. McNamara retorted testily that the woman could easily have found one of her arms ripped off for a leopard snack. The woman protested that the leopard had been at the other side of the cage and she would have pulled her arms away in time if she had been attacked.

Not surprisingly, this woman had been drinking. McNamara called the police and had her escorted from the zoo.

One side effect of our modern society is that the average American has no clue what wild animals are capable of. McNamara was certainly correct about a snow leopard's abilities to move swiftly and silently. There have been cases where keepers have been killed or severely crippled by their charges. For example, at the John Ball Zoo in Grand Rapids back in the 1980s, a jaguar once broke the neck of one of the keepers. This was due to a flaw in the exhibit design that permitted the leopard to hide above the entranceway to the enclosure. When the unsuspecting keeper walked inside to feed the cat, the jaguar's natural instincts took charge. It pounced on her from behind before she saw a thing. More recently, on February 24, 2007, Denver Zoo keeper Ashlee Pfaff mistakenly thought that an exhibit was empty. She entered it and was killed by a jaguar. Such deaths are rare, however, and Pfaff's was the first such incident involving a large cat in over fifteen years.

Fortunately, no zoo keepers or other staff members at Potter Park Zoo have ever been killed. That does not mean there haven't been some close calls. Interestingly, those close calls have frequently been the result of herbivore attacks, not carnivores as one might suspect.

A camel was the culprit in one case. This particular species has an earned reputation for being very obstinate at times. Usually, this is just unpleasant, such as when a camel spits half-digested cud and saliva into your face in a big glob of green, noxious goo. One day in May of 1997, however, a camel named Gloria became upset when a young keeper's assistant, Stephanie Lynn, insisted Gloria go into a building for the night. Gloria wanted to stay outside and eat, however, and when Stephanie accidentally slipped while trying to move the camel, Gloria decided to sit on her. This might sound humorous at first, but poor Stephanie found herself completely buried under the camel's belly and couldn't breathe. The staff quickly ran to help her, as did an assistant cub scout master named Anne Hodge, who overheard screaming and rushed to help. Heaving and pushing the camel with all their might, they were able to extricate Stephanie, who suffered a dislocated hip.[5] Fortunately, speedy medical attention was applied and she recovered fully. Still, the zoo decided to discontinue the camel rides not long after that, and Gloria was shipped back to her owner in Kokomo, Indiana. The rides were reinstated in 2004 when the zoo hired a new independent vendor who takes care that the camels are handled only by herself and her employees.

Another unhappy occurrence was experienced by Jan Brigham, who in 1995 or 1996 (she couldn't recall the exact year) was attacked by the ironically named Cupid the Reindeer. He was named that because he was born on February 14. Cupid was two years old at the time, which meant he was sexually mature and becoming very protective of his harem of cows. The keepers had noticed his increasing aggression, which was further stimulated by the sounds of the rakes and shovels they used that may have sounded a little to a reindeer like clashing antlers. Brigham, being an experienced keeper by then, was noticing subtle behavioral changes in Cupid, a sure warning sign that something was up.

Brigham came in early on a September morning to bottle feed a baby moose and a baby zebu that were under the zoo's care then. "I walked into the reindeer yard with my bucket of food, and the first thing that I noticed was that Cupid was starting to come toward me and not keep his females down at one end [something that he had been doing previously], so I knew that there was a problem, and that I needed to just dump the food into the nearest food dish and then get out of there because he had changed his behavior. So, I did, but he was too quick. He ended up charging me, lifted me up on his antlers, and then he like put me back down on the ground and bulldozed me around on the ground. I really figured at that point that I was probably dead, or was going to be. But he stopped and I was just literally screaming for help!"[6] A maintenance man named Rob Pfund ran to her aid. A man of only about four-and-a-half feet in height, Pfund grabbed one of Cupid's antlers while Brigham held onto the other.

They were both dragged around the yard by the powerful bull reindeer. Brigham was able to get out, and when Cupid rammed the fence, she grabbed an antler, pulled hard, and gave Pfund time to flee as well. Brigham suffered from a punctured leg, but thankfully nothing more serious. That was the third time Brigham had been attacked by a male deer species.

ANIMAL CONTROL

Incidents such as these make animal control an important aspect of the keeper's job. Wild animals, as the term implies, do not really belong in limited enclosures. It is a sad fact of reality that today's zoos play a necessary role in animal conservation, and thus these zoo animals—which I like to call "Ambassadors of the Wild Kingdom" because they are important representatives for their species—must remain in zoos. In some cases, zoos are the only places left in the world for them to exist.

The very nature of zoo exhibits, no matter how accommodating and realistic they are designed to be for the animals' comfort, is restrictive. Therefore, these creatures often either behave in ways that are not really natural for them (e.g., repetitive behaviors, such as pac-

The guinea pig mound, which was once located near where the penguin exhibit is today, was the victim of monkey raids on more than one occasion (photo courtesy Potter Park Zoo).

Escapes at the zoo are rare, but they do happen. "Lester" the spider monkey made an infamous attempt in 1976. Unfortunately, he was electrocuted while swinging on power lines. Monkey Island proved unsuitable for containing primate species, which is why they are now in much more secure exhibits (photo courtesy Potter Park Zoo).

ing), or they try to behave so naturally that it makes them difficult to control. The best example of the latter is the animal escape. There have been a number of times over the years where animals have found ways to break out of their enclosures. Though a serious concern for keepers, at times this can be somewhat amusing.

Monkey species, being so clever, are notorious for wreaking havoc. Before the spider monkeys were placed on Monkey Island (now the Big Horn sheep exhibit), there were rhesus monkeys there for a time while the zoo was taking care of a control population of the species for a research project being run by the state's health lab (located where the company BioPort is now). Bill Swix recalled some odd behavior from them: "The rhesus monkeys were jumping off the island and coming over and picking up the guinea pigs, and they'd take them over there [back to Monkey Island] and pull their hair out and put them back in their display! So we had some bald guinea pigs running around!"[7] Interestingly, the monkeys were not trying to escape, because they always returned to the island: they were just seeking some entertainment.

The rhesus monkeys also caused the City Council some grief. Council members were holding a barbeque at the park one night when another monkey escaped the island and stole their steaks. "After that there were no more rhesus monkeys on the island," laughed Swix. Since rhesus monkeys are more agile than spider monkeys, they could not be kept on the island.

Most people believe that zoo animals flee their exhibits because they wish to somehow return to their natural habitats. Actually, it is often simply because they are restless or curious. Since they have a reliable supply of food at the zoo and a safe place to sleep, most wildlife ambassadors are perfectly happy to stay at the zoo. As a docent, I am often asked, for example, about Potter Park's peafowl, which are allowed to roam the grounds at will. "Why don't they leave the zoo?" a child will inquire. Well, it's simply because they know they can eat all they want at the zoo! Also, the zoo grounds are plenty large enough for their territorial needs, so there's no compelling reason to leave (although the peafowl have been known to wander outside the zoo's gates).

A good example of one animal leaving the zoo and coming back is Aspen the Arctic fox vixen. Aspen was often used in zoo education programs and was very comfortable with humans, but one day in 1990 she escaped her exhibit by tunneling under three fences. Kelliann Whitney, who was education curator at the time and knew Aspen well, thought that the fox was surely gone for good. The next day, she was running an errand at a Kinko's store when she saw Aspen trotting down the street. She called to the vixen, and Aspen came running up to her. "I just scooped her up and took her back to the zoo," Whitney said.[8]

Unfortunately, the repercussions of an animal escape are not always so happy. For example, a monkey once escaped Monkey Island only to be electrocuted when it climbed on some power lines near the zoo. One of the worst escapes to happen at a zoo occurred on Christmas Day 2007, at the San Francisco Zoo, when a tiger named Tatiana managed to climb over the walls and fencing and attack three young men. Seventeen-year-old Carlos Sousa Jr. was mauled to death, and his two friends, Amritpal (Paul) Dhaliwal (nineteen years old) and Kulbir Dhaliwal (twenty-three) were seriously injured. In the aftermath, it was widely reported that the young men had taunted the tiger, using slingshots to shoot sticks and pine cones into the exhibit[9] and provoking the huge cat to perform a physical feat beyond what exhibit designers expected from the Siberian tiger. Although they denied wrongdoing, the two surviving men were also accused of being high on vodka and marijuana that day.

Because escapes are potentially hazardous to the public, the zoo staff, or the animals themselves, these incidents are taken very seriously by Potter Park Zoo. Today, regular drills are held at the zoo at least four times a year to make sure everyone is prepared for such an occurrence. Working with Lansing's police and fire departments, the zoo staff simulates an animal escape to practice procedures. These days, the role of the animal is played by Education Curator Dennis Laidler or an intern, who then has the interesting job of carrying a mock animal around (such as a plaster deer used by hunters for target practice) and running around within or outside the zoo grounds until he can be found and "recaptured" by the staff.

Exhibit design, as one might imagine, is very important as well in keeping animals within their enclosures. Improvements over the years have greatly reduced escape incidents at Potter Park Zoo.

WHY DO KEEPERS LIKE THEIR TOUGH JOBS?

With all the hard—and often disagreeable—work, fairly unextraordinary pay (though being unionized helps), and frustrations in being a zoo keeper, one might ask, "Why do they do it?" The only possible answer, of course, is the love and respect for wildlife that keepers nurture in their hearts. Zoo keeping is an emotionally and psychologically rewarding job, knowing that one is playing an important role in helping these animals, many of whom have nowhere else to go in a world where natural habitats are quickly being destroyed by human overpopulation.

Longtime keeper Jan Brigham explained her passion for the job this way:

> There is always something different happening at the zoo. It may be an animal birth or death, an acquisition of a new animal or disposition of one of our animals to another zoo, working with teen keepers

Being a zoo keeper isn't *all* work; it can be a lot of fun, too! Here, keepers Janice Tomlian and Mark Marquardt teach Ebony the rhino to paint with her lip as an enrichment activity (photo courtesy Potter Park Zoo).

or MSU interns, or watching the vet do a procedure. I like the fact that my job is somewhat unpredictable. I like interacting with the visitors; it gives me the chance to educate people about the animals I take care of. I like the fact that my job is physical and keeps me in good shape. I like working outdoors. Most of all, I like the animals.

The most memorable and rewarding experience I have had at Potter Park Zoo is being midwife to a llama. One of our llamas was giving birth and the presentation of the baby was incorrect. Only the nose was showing when we should have also been seeing the two front feet. I called Dr. Sikarskie and told him the llama was having a birthing problem. He explained to me over the phone that I should wash up and put my arms into the birth canal and find the feet so that the baby was positioned properly for delivery. I had never done anything like this before, but I found this procedure absolutely fascinating. I reached into the birth canal and was able to unfold the legs so the feet were in proper position. After taking my arms out, the llama was able to deliver her baby successfully. The very next year she experienced something similar and I was very confident that I could help her again, which I did.

Keeper Sarah Foote helps hand raise a cotton-top tamarin monkey that was rejected by its parents (photo by Kevin Hile).

Hand raising baby animals sounds like it would be a wonderful job, and it is to a certain extent. When we were bottle feeding the tiger cubs born in 2006, we had to come in every two to three hours all night for the first week. That schedule gets old fast when you have to leave your house and travel to the zoo to do the feedings.

Janice Tomlian delivers a newborn muntjac baby (photo courtesy Potter Park Zoo).

> Sometimes the tiger cubs weren't cooperative, but in the end the hard work done by a number of keepers and our vet was well worth the trouble.[10]

Sometimes, keepers can become very attached to their charges. This has been especially true with some of Potter Park's more charismatic animals, such as Herman and Bingo, and it can be easy to anthropomorphize such animals. Keepers and volunteers at the zoo are always instructed to tell visitors that these are wild animals, not pets. Yet keepers often name the animals that are most memorable to them, and the public wants to associate names with many of these creatures as well. Sometimes, the names keepers give animals and the names the general public knows aren't even the same. For example, the female black rhino at the zoo is known as "Rafiki" to the public, but the zoo keepers call her "Ebony" because that was the name she had when she arrived at Potter Park Zoo. In official record keeping, this is known as the animal's "house name." A lot of animals are given house names that the public doesn't know about. For example, all the wallabies at the zoo currently have names given to them by the keepers, but they are anonymous to most visitors who are more excited about the megavertebrates, such as the tigers.

Target training takes a lot of time and work, but it is a fascinating part of a keeper's job to modify an animal's behavior so that veterinarians and other staff can work with the animal safely (photo courtesy Potter Park Zoo).

Giving animals such as Bingo names is also helpful in terms of promotional efforts and public relations. The AZA has gone back and forth on this issue over the years. Back in the 1990s, they discouraged giving animals names so that it could be emphasized that they were wild creatures and not pets or objects for people's amusement. More recently, however, the AZA has recognized the futility of such a policy, as well as the benefits of allowing the general public to feel emotional attachments toward animals. This, it is hoped, will help people care more about wildlife conservation.

Gerry Brady takes this a step further by holding animal naming competitions where the public can submit name proposals for newborns at the zoo. Winners are picked by the staff, the announcement is made to the local news media, and voilá: instant publicity!

THE FIRST LINE OF DEFENSE

No one knows and understands the animals at Potter Park Zoo better than the keepers. Because they work with these wild kingdom

A teen keeper works behind the scenes at the Bird/Reptile House (photo by Kevin Hile).

ambassadors day in and day out, they are familiar with them not only from a general, scientific view of their basic needs and care, but also on an individual level. Animals, like people, have unique personalities. All lions are not alike, nor are all tigers, pandas, monkeys, or llamas. It is the keepers who can pick out very subtle changes in each animal's behavior, appearance, and even their smell. As Mary Anne McNamara noted, sometimes a keeper can just walk into an exhibit and immediately sense that something is wrong. Therefore, they are the first to decide when to alert the zoo's veterinarian. When time is critical, this can be particularly important. Even though Potter Park now has an on-grounds, full-time veterinarian in Dr. Tara Harrison, she is only one individual who can't possibly keep track of all that's going on in the collection by herself.

As McNamara emphasized, even when a keeper is simply feeding the animals, observation is key: "You have to look at every animal. You don't just walk into a barn in the morning and throw hay in a feed rack and walk out. You have to check.... You have to pay attention to everything about that animal's regular, daily routine, and then it's your job to record it on your daily log, and/or immediately go to your supervisor if there is something that is visibly serious enough right then. You know, something different from when you last saw the animal."

McNamara added that making time for simple observation of animals is something that should be made part of any keeper's routine. Next time you visit a zoo and see a keeper who just seems to be "standing around doing nothing," you'll now know that is definitely not the case!

Once a problem has been identified by a keeper, the vet is contacted, and, depending on what the keeper tells her, will either come out immediately or ask the keeper to keep an eye on the situation and inform her of changes. If medical treatment is needed, keepers also assist the vet in capturing and/or restraining the animal. Their role here, too, is vital, because usually the animals are more familiar with their keepers than the vet, and so they trust them more. Not only that, but animals quite cleverly can associate the vet with unpleasant things, such as needles, so they need the keepers to calm them down and comfort them. Sedation or general anesthesia, when needed, is a very tricky thing to administer, and any vet will tell you that death is always a potential result. Because of this risk, vets prefer to use only tranquilization or a local anesthetic for smaller animals that can be safely restrained. Still, larger animals need to be put completely under for everyone's safety, and keepers help vets to prepare the animals for sedation as best as possible. (It is very risky to anesthetize rhinos, however, so this is avoided whenever possible).

Keepers also advise vets on the best approach to administering a drug or otherwise treating an animal, given that individual's personality or unique physical or medical history. "So you're supposed to know," said McNamara, such facts as "does this animal go into this holding pen easily? If not, then how do I get them in there? Or, here are my options, which of these is going to cause the animal the least stress? Or, at what time of the day would this be best?"

Sometimes, several keepers are needed in order to handle an animal, such as one time in the early 1980s that McNamara recalled when they had to carry a male tapir that had become ill. Rolled onto a tarp, it took ten staff, including keepers and maintenance people, to carry the beast, which weighed about 700 pounds.

On the happier occasions of animal births, keepers are also the ones who tend to the infants, especially when they have to be hand-raised. This sometimes happens when a mother, for one reason or another, rejects one or more of her babies. Keepers then have to bottle feed these babies, which is a twenty-four-hour-a-day job. There have been a number of times, as well, when a vet was not immediately available, that a keeper had to serve as midwife and deliver an animal safely.

Midwives, nurses, adoptive parents, EMT crews, wildlife observers, even anesthesiologists, when called for: keepers serve all these functions. The combination of a good education and extensive experience makes the keepers at Potter Park Zoo indispensable participants in the mission of conservation.

Keepers are often the first on hand to inform the zoo vet when an animal is about to give birth. The author was fortunate enough to be at the zoo, too, when this bactrian camel was born in 2005 (photos by Kevin Hile).

8

Science at Potter Park Zoo

As the world's human population has grown exponentially through the twentieth century and into the twenty-first, the planet has become a crowded place. Habitat destruction for the sake of building homes and businesses for *Homo sapiens* has meant that animals are quickly running out of places to live. For wildlife, this has contributed to the current mass extinction in which the rate animals are disappearing on the planet is a thousand times that of a natural extinction rate, according to the United Nations report *Global Biodiversity Outlook 2* released in 2006.[1] It is an event quietly going on in the background of our lives that some scientists say is responsible for the extinction of at least one hundred species *per year,* which is comparable to the previous mass extinction sixty-five million years ago that marked the demise of dinosaurs. While we go to work, eat, sleep, play, and spend time with friends and family, species are disappearing at the rate of one every three or four *days*!

Threats to Wildlife

It's not easy being a wild animal these days. There are so many threats to wildlife—most of them caused by human beings—that in some ways it is a wonder they survive at all. Below is a list of some of the major reasons why animals become threatened, endangered, or extinct.

- Habitat destruction
- Pollution
- Overhunting/overfishing
- Poaching (for meat, fur, feathers, shells, body parts used for traditional medicines, or other animal parts used for decorations or household items)
- Competition from non-native species
- Disease spread by non-native or domestic species
- Rapid environmental changes (e.g., global warming, damming of rivers, suburban sprawl)
- The exotic pet trade
- War (people aren't the only victims)

Most people on the planet are unaware of this tragedy, yet it goes on every day as forests are chopped down, coral reefs die off from bleaching caused by global warming, and poachers and pollution kill off the rest.

It has only been over the last few decades that this fact has really hit home at zoos. Once, zoos were able to capture the animals they needed in the wild and transport them to the United States for display. Around the 1970s, people began to notice that it was becoming very difficult to continue this practice. The animals were no longer there to be found! Thus, the role of zoos began to change. The new mission of wildlife conservation became the purpose for many zoos; the AZA began the Species Survival Plan, and at the same time national and international laws were being written to protect rare and endangered species of all kinds.

An immediate effect on zoos was a dawning awareness that it had become even more important to keep their existing animals alive and to breed them successfully.

PARTNERING WITH MSU

Michigan State University once provided veterinary services to the zoo gratis. Although they did not receive a fee, the vets and vet students were repaid by gaining valuable experience treating exotic animals they would likely never otherwise see. Unfortunately, when the university downsized the veterinary school's budget, they had to start charging the zoo for their services in the 1990s. This became increasingly expensive, and when the AZA inspected Potter Park Zoo for its 2001 reaccreditation, they insisted that the zoo hire an on-staff, full-time veterinarian. This led to the hiring of Dr. Tara Myers Harrison in 2003.

However, the relationship with MSU's vet school is still strong. Dr. Harrison often calls upon their services to assist with procedures that require more than one vet, or to seek their input on diagnoses or other medical matters.

One important example of this partnership with MSU vets was the Bingo operation. Though Bingo passed away, a great deal was learned from that experience that could be put to good use should other similar cases arise at other zoos.

In addition to surgeries, professors and students have aided Potter Park in scientific research that has been of great benefit to zoo animals across the country. A good example of that involves the area of nutrition.

ZOO ANIMAL NUTRITION

For Americans, dietary health has been very much in the news for many years, especially with regard to obesity, junk food, and processed foods, all of which can lead to everything from heart disease to diabetes to cancer. Remarkably, the same concern for a balanced diet has received much less attention in zoos, according to Dr. Duane Ullrey, who is now a professor emeritus at MSU's Departments of Animal Science and Fisheries and Wildlife. He has done work as a consultant for the zoo as far back as 1968. Although he maintains that zoo nutrition is a very basic science that one would think would be central to animal care, there is not enough training given to vets as there should be, nor is it emphasized enough at zoos, large or small. In the best of worlds, commented Dr. Ullrey, all zoos should not only have a full-time vet, but also an on-staff animal nutritionist. "The reason for that," he said, "is that they need to work together because nutrition is the most basic part of husbandry and is basic to animal health."[2]

One of the first studies Dr. Ullrey did at Potter Park was for the zoo's wolves. The grey wolves were being fed a soft diet of ground meat, which encouraged the buildup of plaque and tartar on their

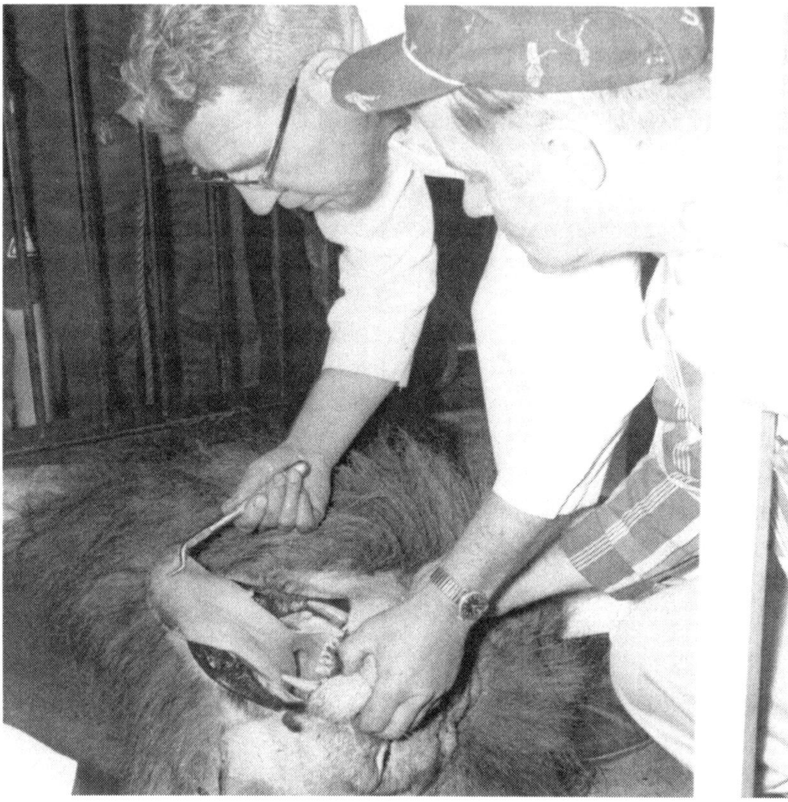

A vet from MSU works on a lion's teeth while zoo manager Ted Downey watches in this undated photo from the 1960s (photo courtesy Maisie Downey).

teeth. Anyone who owns a dog or cat knows that tartar (also called calculus), if unchecked, can lead to other health problems, and Ullrey got the zoo staff to switch to a crunchy dog food to help clean their teeth. Bones are also an important part of any carnivore diet, and so they are given to animals such as the lions and tigers once a week to help keep their teeth clean.

Dr. Ullrey was not alone in his work at Potter Park Zoo, however. His student, Dr. Mark Edwards, did much of his early research at Lansing's zoo and became a prominent wildlife nutritionist. He later worked at the San Diego Zoo for about a decade and is now on staff at the National Zoo in Washington, D.C.

The fundamental problem of zoo diets is that it is nearly impossible to replicate the plants and meats that these animals would normally eat in the wild. In Africa, a lion pride will tackle a zebra and

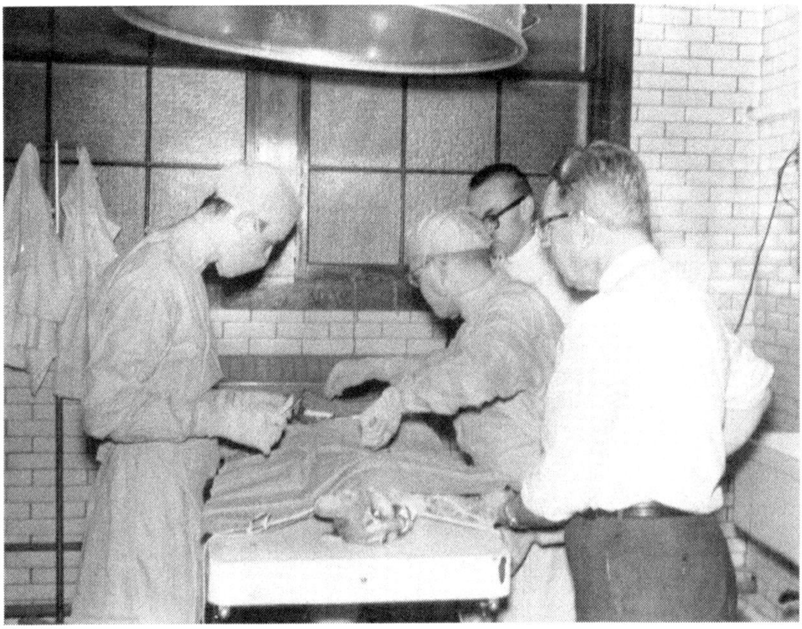

A cougar is operated on at the MSU College of Veterinary Medicine in this undated photo. The university and zoo have enjoyed a long partnership over the decades (photo courtesy Maisie Downey).

devour it completely within hours, including internal organs, tendons, and bits of hide. Even a herbivore's food can be problematic. For example, black rhinos browse a variety of leafy and woody plants, as well as some fruits that are native to Africa but not readily available in the United States. In captivity they eat hay, monogastric pellets, and treats such as apples, carrots, and bananas. It's not exactly the same food, but it would be too expensive and laborious to ship in the exact same vegetables a rhino eats in the wild, and it's not too likely that zoos are going to allow their lions to munch on the zebra collection. Still, zoo staff do the best they can, adding variety when it is available.

Sometimes that variety presents itself conveniently. There have been many instances when squirrels, rabbits, birds, and other native Michigan animals have wandered into a wolf or snow leopard exhibit only to find themselves turned into a snack. Just a couple of months ago, for instance, I watched as one of the yearling tiger cubs chased a sparrow around its exhibit. The little bird offered several minutes of amusement before it became an hors d'oeuvre.

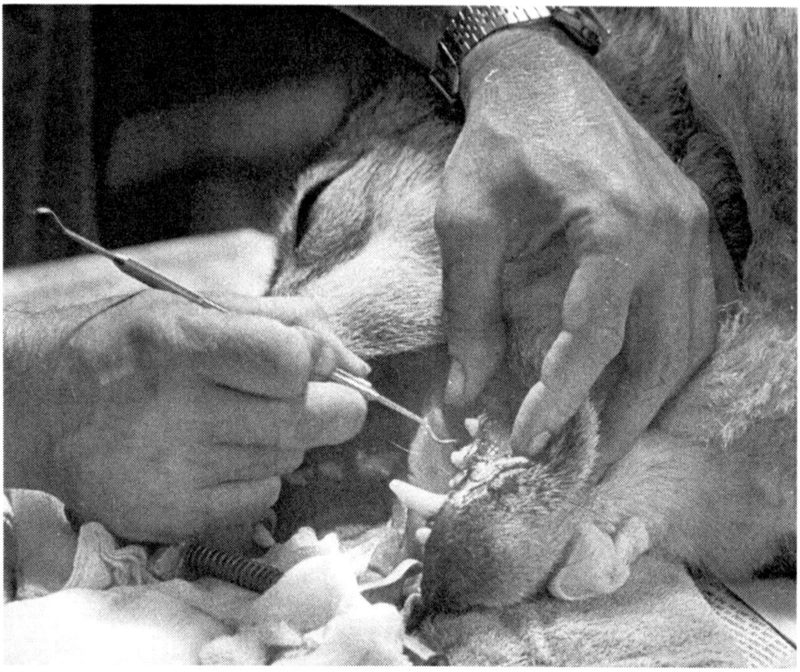

A timber wolf has plaque removed while under anesthesia at MSU. Diets at the zoo have changed for many animals to improve their dental health—and their health in general (photo by Norris Ingells courtesy Melissa Ingells).

Food Consumption at Potter Park Zoo (2005)*

One question visitors regularly ask docents at the zoo is how much do the animals eat? Well, quite a bit! Below is a table showing just how much food was consumed by Potter Park Zoo's animals in 2005.

Type of Food	Amount
Alfalfa	350 bales
Grass Hay	1,700 bales
Carnivore Diet	7,200 lbs.
Knuckle Bones	600 lbs.
Capelin (fish)	5,798 lbs.
Smelt (fish)	55 lbs.
Herring (fish)	750 lbs.
Jalapeno Peppers	3 lbs.
Red Grapes	251 lbs.
Turnip Greens	35 cases

Type of Food	Amount
Potato Yams	181 lbs.
Oranges	349 ea.
Green Peppers	148 ea.
Cucumbers	68 ea.
Tomatoes	121 lbs.
Squash Zucchinis	11 lbs.
Cantaloupes	29 ea.
Onions	102 lbs.
Broccoli	86 ea.
Celery	71 ea.
Red Delicious Apples	2,700 ea.
Bananas	510 lbs.
Carrots	340 lbs.
Summer Squash	3 lbs.
Cabbage Slaw (w/carrots)	20 lbs.
Limes	42 ea.
Lettuce	8 ea.
White Potatoes	60 lbs.
Lemons	18 ea.
Collard Greens	14 cases
Crickets	120,000 ea.
Wax Worms	9,000-12,000 ea.
Meal Worms	12,000-24,000 ea.

*Source: Potter Park Zoo

Food supplements are essential in order to more closely mimic the vitamins and minerals these animals should be getting. This is important for reasons other than health, too. Animal coloring, for example, can be dependent on diet, especially in the case of birds. What's in their food contributes to plumage coloration. Although there are no flamingoes at Potter Park, they are an excellent example of this: the pink in flamingo feathers depends on eating shrimp. Again, most zoos don't even try to ship in the shrimp they need, so instead the birds are given supplements that contain the appropriate chemicals that occur naturally in the shrimp.

Of special concern to zoos is the diet of newborn animals. This is especially true when a mother rejects an infant and the animal needs to be hand raised. Mother's milk varies from species to species, and each type of animal requires different vitamins, fats, proteins, and even bacteria to grow up healthy. For example, in raising tiger cubs, vets and zoo keepers counter-intuitively learned that these young cats did better on a meal of milk formulated for puppies than they did on milk for kittens. At the Detroit Zoo, it was learned that kangaroo joeys must ingest some of their mother's feces in order to have the needed bacteria in their stomachs to process plant roughage when they are weaned off their mother's milk.

Ullrey, whose education includes degrees in husbandry, pathology, and animal nutrition, stresses that the decisions zoos make in feeding their animals should not be made lightly. "We have a choice [in what we eat], you see. Animals don't when they're in captivity. They're given the option of eating what they're presented with, and if the choices are inappropriate, then they suffer the consequences."

Fighting Off Disease

Another challenge of transplanting exotics to a zoo in Michigan is disease. The risk is not so much that the non-endemic species might bring an illness into the country (new arrivals are always placed in quarantine for several weeks and given thorough exams to make sure they are disease free) but in the diseases that they are exposed to while here—or illnesses that they may have contracted while traveling to Michigan—against which they might not have the needed immunity.

In 2002 this was made blatantly apparent when West Nile virus invaded Michigan. Many birds, and some hoof stock species, are particularly vulnerable to this virus—most notably, snowy owls. The disease quickly killed both the female and male owls at the zoo in Lansing, and, indeed, across the country. Snowy owls, whose habitat in the far north meant they had never been exposed to this warm-climate disease, had no antibodies to kill the virus, so the deadly flu it inspired killed off many of them that were living in zoos.

The zoo's penguins suffered as well. Apparently, however, they did not die from the West Nile virus directly; instead, it is theorized that the virus weakened their immune systems, which allowed another disease common in penguins in North American zoos, aspergillosis, to spread wildly in their systems. At Potter Park, this meant that all but one of the Magellanic penguins perished. Fortunately, the one that survived was the most valuable genetically, yet it was still a sharp blow to the zoo. West Nile is typically spread by mosquitoes, and so mosquito control has become an important task at the zoo. This is largely done by eliminating standing water and spreading larvalcides to kill mosquitoes before they reach adulthood.

Other animals who come unwanted to the zoo are equally dangerous. Squirrels can spread mange, for instance, but the two worst culprits are raccoons and stray cats. Raccoons, which are extremely common in the wooded areas of Potter Park, spread canine distemper and balyisascaris, the latter being a parasitic roundworm "that in the wrong animal can basically create highways in the brain,"[3] according to Dr. Tara Harrison, the zoo's vet. In other words, they burrow through an animal's grey matter.

Domestic cats, which many people wrongfully believe should be allowed to wander freely through neighborhoods, can spread a lethal disease called toxoplasmosis. More recently, Potter Park had the dubious distinction of being the first zoo in the country to have a tiger die as a result of feline calicivirus (FCV). This virus, common in domestic cats, typically only manifests itself as a mild to strong cold. However, in March 2005, a mother Amur tiger at the zoo and her four cubs suffered a virulent outbreak of FCV. One cub, a male, died of the disease, while the others were able to be nursed to health and today are doing well. A cat was captured outside the Feline/Primate House and tested positive for the virus. Dr. Harrison suspects that it might be a new, more malignant mutation of the FCV virus, or that there was an increase in susceptibility to the virus for some unknown reason. It is also possible that the vaccines that vets used for domestic cats don't work on tigers or other exotic cats. (Research is currently in progress to evaluate this). This would explain why the big cats, which had all been inoculated for the normal form of FCV, became sick. It is possible, she speculates, that the cat spread the disease to the weakened immune system of the zoo's male lion, Samburu. At the time, the lion was being treated with chemotherapy for cancer, which likely weakened his immunity and caused him to contract FCV, which was then spread to the tigers. This means there is yet another potential threat to zoo animals to be considered in the future.

From Routine to Groundbreaking Medicine

Being a small zoo with a limited budget is a disadvantage for Dr. Harrison. "The challenge that we have is that I don't have any help *per se*, like any veterinary technicians or anything like that, so I'm all on my own. I can get help, but that just means that I call MSU and I

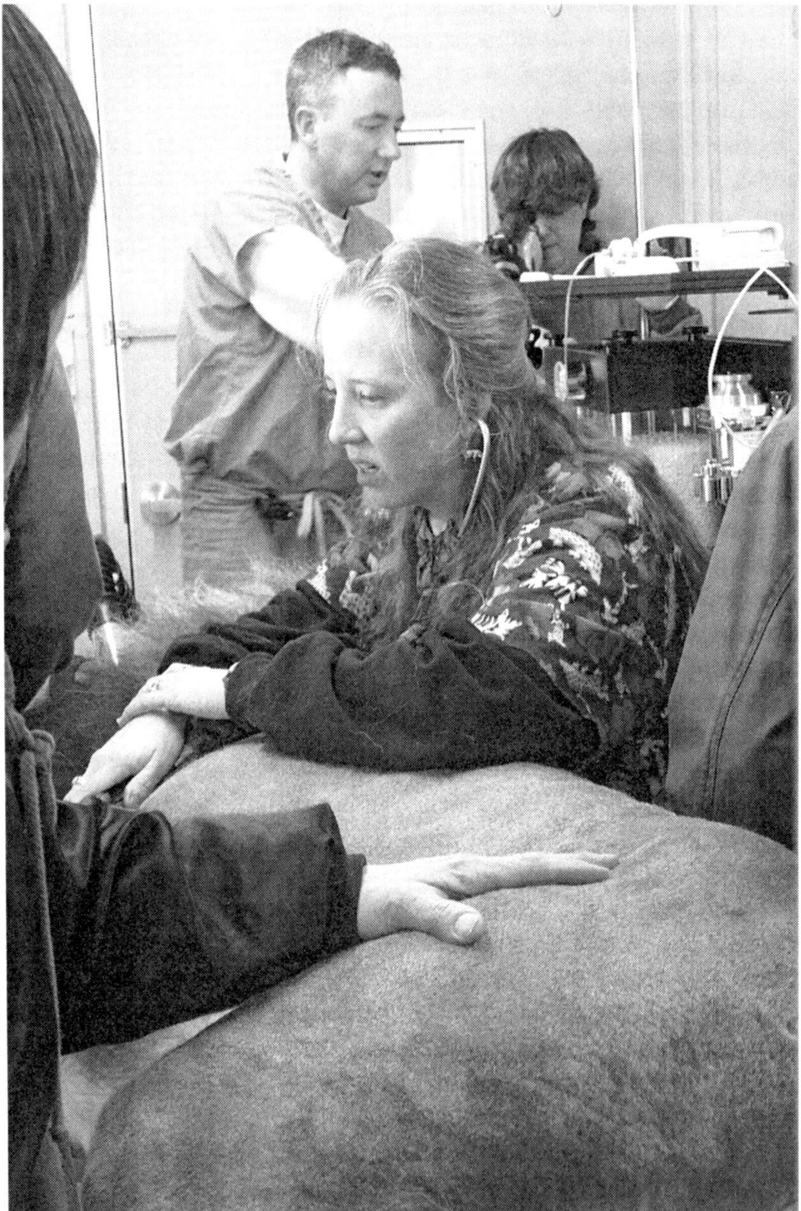

Dr. Tara Harrison checks Samburu's heart just before the male African lion underwent groundbreaking surgery to remove a tumor from his spleen (photo courtesy Potter Park Zoo).

Thanks to his successful surgery, Samburu lived another healthy eighteen months, finally passing away at a ripe old age in 2005 (photo by David Mills courtesy Potter Park Zoo Society).

beg. So, that's the biggest challenge here is the lack of support staff. Whereas at a bigger zoo you'll have six veterinarians, ten veterinary technicians, and a couple of assistants." Fortunately, professors at

Small animals pose particularly difficult challenges during operations, simply because the anatomy is on such a small scale. Here, Dr. Harrison operates on a massasauga rattlesnake (photo courtesy Potter Park Zoo).

MSU have proven generous with their time. More than fifteen professors in the College of Veterinary Medicine regularly performed *pro bono* work for the zoo in 2005.

Being a zoo veterinarian anywhere, for that matter, is a challenge. As Dr. Harrison pointed out, veterinary science is still a discipline in its infancy. "We only have five books written" on zoo medicine, commented Harrison. Consequently, much of the work she does at Potter Park has never been done anywhere before. This was certainly the case with the FCV cases. When Dr. Harrison called the vet school at MSU, as well as other zoos, to try to get some advice on how to proceed, professors and other doctors had no idea what to tell her; it was an unprecedented situation. So, she had to treat the tiger cubs based on what was already known about FCV and hope for the best.

When Samburu developed cancer in 2003, Dr. Tara, along with assisting medical professionals from MSU, including Dr. Sikarskie and several others, performed the first-ever successful splenectomy and chemotherapy on a lion. Removing the cancerous spleen and treating Samburu with chemotherapy gave the fourteen-year-old lion an additional eighteen months of life, during most of which he enjoyed a good quality of life, a healthy appetite, and maintained his notoriously tough attitude toward the keepers.

Some large animals, such as the rhinos, have to be treated within their exhibits because of their size. Others that are easier to transport, however, are taken to Potter Park Zoo's new Animal Clinic. Formerly the building that housed the animals used for the Society's education programs, the Clinic was completely renovated in 2002, thanks to a $50,000 grant from the Rotary Club of Lansing. Now housing an operating table, autoclave, X-ray machine and developer, microscope and other equipment, some of which was generously donated by Sparrow Hospital and the Animal Emergency Hospital of Grand Rapids, the new clinic makes it possible to perform medical procedures without transporting animals to MSU for surgery.

In addition to the lion splenectomy, many other interesting procedures have been performed at Potter Park Zoo in recent years. Among these are root canals on the river otters (compliments of the skilled hands of Dr. Richard Stillwill), bladder surgery on an Arctic fox, evaluating tissue samples from lemurs to study their genetics, and the artificial insemination of a bongo. The first two procedures on the bongo unfortunately did not result in a pregnancy, but the staff is still hoping

Dr. Harrison draws blood from a rhino. Some animals at the zoo, such as rhinos, are so large that it is easier to treat them in their exhibits (photo courtesy Potter Park Zoo).

The new Animal Clinic was renovated in 2002. Plans are in the works for another expansion (photo by Kevin Hile).

to try again. While these artificial insemination trials are important for science, it should be pointed out that Potter Park Zoo has also been successful in breeding bongos through natural means, which is just one of many significant achievements the zoo can claim in preserving such endangered species.

Artificial insemination is one cutting-edge piece of science that Potter Park Zoo and other zoos around the country hope will save critically endangered species from going extinct. There are several zoos around the country that have "frozen zoos." These are zoos that can actually store the eggs, sperm, and even embryos of various animals. Among the dozen or so frozen zoos operating around the world are those at the San Diego and Cincinnati Zoos. When Potter Park lost its breeding fishing cat, the cat's extremely valuable oocyctes were collected and frozen in the hopes that they could still be fertilized and implanted into a surrogate fishing cat.

RESEARCH AND CONSERVATION

Staff, students, and even volunteers are involved in work that zoo visitors never see, yet it is an essential part of the mission of conservation. Before people can save animals from extinction, they must understand not only their physiology and dietary needs, but also their behavior in the wild. Dr. Tara Harrison and Potter Park Zoo are currently involved in many research projects. For example, the MSU Department of Fisheries and Wildlife is working with the zoo to put radio transmitters on native Michigan Massasauga rattlesnakes (in 2008, fox snakes were added to the study). By studying their movements, scientists will better understand their natural ranges and where they most like to live; in this way, we will know which areas are critical rattlesnake habitat that should be preserved from development, thus doing a great deal to insure the rattlesnake's survival.

SSP Animals at Potter Park Zoo

As of 2008, Potter Park Zoo was taking care of the following species that are part of the Species Survival Plan:

- African lion
- Amur tigers
- Bali mynah birds
- Black rhinos*
- Bongos
- Cotton-top tamarin monkeys
- Golden lion tamarin monkeys
- Kingfisher
- Mandrills
- Mongoose lemurs
- Red pandas
- Ring-tailed lemurs
- River otters
- Scimitar-horned oryx
- Snow leopards
- Spider monkeys

*Temporarily off exhibit in 2008, black rhinos might be replaced by white rhinos at the zoo.

Potter Park is also working with the Smithsonian Institute, White Oak Plantation, and the University of Florida on a black rhinoceros research project; Dr. Harrison is continuing her FCV study (which will be coordinated with zoos across the United States) and research on lymphoma in lions, a project started with Samburu's cancer.

Target training of the tiger cubs has been very useful for the zoo's veterinarian, as well. As Dr. Harrison related: "Our tiger cubs are

Because of successful target training, Dr. Harrison was able to extract blood samples from the zoo's three tiger cubs, performing useful blood value evaluations that had never before been conducted (photo courtesy Potter Park Zoo).

being studied to evaluate their blood values (glucose, white cell count, etc.) and blood pressure when they're awake because we don't have any blood values or blood pressure for tigers that are awake; we just have them all when they're under anesthesia." In other words, understanding the actual waking state of a tiger's blood will help veterinarians identify illness in a tiger more quickly. How do vets take blood samples from a conscious tiger? Very carefully. Well, actually, the answer is target training. Through painstaking training efforts over the course of weeks and months, tigers and snow leopards at the zoo are conditioned so that they tolerate being weighed, presenting their paws for blood extraction, and even submitting to ultrasounds. This proved critical in 2006 for the female snow leopard. Veterinarians were able to determine she had two cubs in her uterus. After giving birth to one cub, the snow leopard developed some pregnancy complications, but since the staff knew there was another cub, a caesarean section was performed. The cub seemed to be dead at first, but it was revived; sadly, it remained weak and did not survive. Without the ultrasound, the body of the cub would have remained inside the womb and likely would have killed the mother. Unfortunately, the other cub died as well, which is not an uncommon occurrence in a first pregnancy for a snow leopard. Despite this outcome, it could have been worse had the mother died as well. Target training saved the day, and the female leopard remains healthy enough to potentially be a mother in the future.

Other people at the zoo are also getting into the act. For example, one of the keepers, Jackie Broder, is conducting a study on binturongs in the area of scent desensitization, and volunteer Jill Garnett is studying enrichment activities in golden lion tamarins.

Tigers are currently the favorite animal at Potter Park Zoo (according to a recent Web site survey), and the zoo is proud of the fact that Gerry Brady is in charge of the Sumatran tiger SSP. This means that it is his responsibility to work with zoos around the country—and around the world—to keep a viable breeding population in captivity. He also does considerable research on tigers and works with foreign governments and zoos as an advisor. This means that Brady takes frequent trips to Southeast Asia, where he has worked to help conservation efforts in Indonesia. He does not limit himself to Sumatran tigers, however, also being concerned with the other four remaining subspecies of tiger: the Siberian, Bengal, Indo-Chinese, and South China tigers.

Primates such as this golden lion tamarin monkey are given food puzzles to solve. Such enrichment items mimic the challenges of finding food in the wild (photo by Jill Garnett courtesy Potter Park Zoo Society).

A snow leopard munches on a pumpkin to get treats inside. Enrichment items such as this help keep zoo animals active and stimulated (photo by Jill Garnett courtesy Potter Park Zoo Society).

Enrichment at the zoo is its own unique field of animal care. For most of Potter Park Zoo's history, providing more than food, shelter, and veterinary care was beyond the means of the zoo's budget and staff time. Thanks to Society volunteers led by Garnett, enrichment has now become a weekly part of the zoo's routine. Enrichments are activities designed to stimulate an animal's natural behaviors—such as foraging for food—which they might not otherwise demonstrate in a zoo enclosure. Some examples of this are creating treats such as pine cones stuffed with fruit for the porcupines, old Christmas trees thrown into the yak's pen (they thoroughly enjoy tossing trees around and turning them into mulch!), and freezing fish into ice balls, a kind of smelly snow cone that all river otters go gaga over.

Even the zoo's young visitors have gotten into the act by helping with enrichment programs. Participating in such programs as ZooKambi and The Big Zoo Lesson, children have been very helpful in making many of the treats animals enjoy at Potter Park.

9

Education: The Zoo Frontier

Of the four missions of the modern-day zoo—conservation, science, education, and family entertainment—many of those involved with Potter Park Zoo feel that education has become the most vital goal today. All of these goals, of course, are important, but there is a reason for this position. Zoos were originally created as a form of entertainment, using spectacular, rarely seen animals to bring wonder into people's lives. But as these animals began disappearing throughout the world, the focus shifted. Zoos realized they would have no animals to show people unless they did something to help endangered species. Science and conservation efforts such as the SSP became key in preserving these animals. But even if zoos were successful in breeding threatened animals and maintaining healthy populations in captivity, what would the future truly be for species such as tigers, rhinos, and elephants? Pretty dismal, unless people throughout the world began to care about their fate.

If no one cares about wildlife, then no one will try to preserve it for future generations to enjoy and appreciate. Because Americans and many other people around the developed world are increasingly alienated from nature, few these days really understand what they are missing. Therefore, it is the job of zoos like Potter Park to tell them about the wonders of the environment and wildlife around them, as well as our dependence upon it.

As Dr. Jim Sikarskie put it, it's difficult to justify keeping animals in captivity without having a real purpose behind it. Some people think this purpose should be conservation, but without any place in the wild to reintroduce many of these animals, the argument for breeding them for the purpose of placing them back where they really belong becomes academic. "It's a very complex issue. The conservation thing is important but it's hard to justify the existence of zoos for recreation and conservation. It's education and research [that are important]."[1]

POTTER PARK'S FIRST EDUCATION EFFORTS

It has only been in the last two decades or so that Potter Park Zoo has been running formal education programs, but long before that Lansing's zoo has served as a resource for students. Located so close to Michigan State University, it was a simple matter for college students of biology and other related areas to visit the zoo and study its animals. For example, Bill Swix noted: "Potter Park Zoo has always been a resource for students writing papers for class. In 1961 I worked with a student who was writing a paper on the evolution of the opposable thumb in primates. Other students wrote papers on social relationships between animals in the zoo displays."[2]

Keepers, as if they did not have enough to do, also volunteered to provide the public, young and old, with guided tours of the zoo. This was not the same as having an education program, however. Therefore, the Friends of the Zoo began contacting local schools in the mid 1970s to invite them to set up field trips. Friends president Ellen Lumbert also was key in helping set up the zoo's first summer school program in 1981. For $10, children ages six through eleven could attend five days of classes, Monday through Friday, for three hours each day. An MSU graduate student in environmental education, Lorraine Austin, was hired by the Friends to teach the classes, which were held at the pavilion by the duck pond. The next year, 1982, a Winter School was introduced that ran every Sunday afternoon.

Austin took a job at Mesker Park Zoo in Evansville, Indiana, in 1984 and, after an interim period led by zoo keeper Jenny Rentfrow, was replaced by a new education curator, Kim Palmer. An MSU junior majoring in communications and environmental sciences at the time, Palmer led what was quickly becoming a growing part of the zoo. The summer program, then called Zoofari, was joined by a program called the Zoo Showcase.

Keeper Jan Brigham teaches students at the zoo in this 1980 photo. Before the zoo began a volunteer docent program, keepers pitched in to help educate the public. In 2008, the zoo added zookeepers back into its educational efforts (photo courtesy Potter Park Zoo).

MSU students continued serving as Education Directors for some time, with Sarah Renton, a graduate of the Fisheries and Wildlife Department at the university, taking the reins in 1985 to head the zoo's classes. During her tenure at Potter Park, the Society initiated its first docent class. Docents, who are now commonly seen at zoos and museums, are ordinary folks who volunteer their free time to educate the public. Trained by Renton, the first class of docents graduated in the spring of 1986 with nine eager volunteers, including future Society directors Carol Webster and Diane McNeil. At the time, there were no formally organized education programs at the zoo, such as tours and school outreaches, but some were soon set up.

The Association of Zoo and Aquarium Docents

Even volunteers at zoos have their own national organization these days. Founded in 1985, the Association of Zoo and Aquarium Docents (AZAD) first met in Houston, Texas. Since then, it has rotated its annual conference sites throughout the United States, bringing together docents, guides, and nature interpreters from all over the world to discuss how they can better themselves as wildlife educators for the public's benefit. Potter Park Zoo's Docent Association sends at least one of its members to the annual conference each year, and usually several other volunteers also attend to bring back what they learned to their colleagues in Lansing. In this way, docents not only bring factual knowledge about wildlife to the public, but also expand their knowledge of teaching techniques to more effectively communicate their message to audiences of all ages.

Ina Martin, who is also the mother of zoo keeper Jan Brigham, was a 1988 graduate of the second docent class (there was no class in 1987), a program she now runs. Martin recalled: "We didn't really have any organized programs at that point. Quite often, I went out with Sarah. A school would call and we would take a little bit of a slide show.... We had a chicken and we had a crow and we had an Arctic fox [this was Aspen] that we took out to schools."[3] Other animals were soon added, however, which brought a lot more variety to the programs.

The "education animals" that went on these trips were kept at various locations around the zoo, including under the Bird/Reptile House and also in the building that was renovated as the Animal Clinic in 2002 in the barnyard area. Rounding up the animals and loading them into their own cars, the docents would travel throughout mid-Michigan. Slowly, they added new species to their list of education animals, including "Sooty" the potbellied pig. Sooty had the honor of sitting in the front seat of the education director's car, riding in style to zoo program destinations.

More and more animals, and more diverse programs, were added over the next couple of years. But because Renton was going to school and running education programs, she really did not have time to dedicate herself fully to the zoo.

EDUCATION TAKES OFF

After Renton left the zoo to focus on her education, the Society hired Kelliann Whitney in 1990. This time, instead of selecting a college student who could not dedicate herself to the job, the Society opted for a full-time employee to be education director. Whitney's previous background was as a monorail guide at the San Diego Wild Animal Park. This was a much more valuable qualification than one might suspect. “It was a wonderful education,” she related. “We had to say something interesting and unusual about 250 different species … in a fifty-minute tour.”[4]

When Whitney arrived, she immediately saw that the education programs needed beefing up. Also, the docents deserved a better education in the science of wildlife. “There was a good docent program in place, but I had very high expectations. Being the only employee in the education department … I knew I wasn’t going to be able to do all of it and do it well.” Thus, classes became much more intense for docents, who received a thorough background in an eight-week course on animal biology, wildlife behavior, ecology, and the environment.

Whitney also improved the summer school program, which she renamed ZooKambi, and added a spring break class that coincided with the public school system’s early year break. Under her guidance, attendance at Potter Park Zoo’s classes grew exponentially. Soon, the program was in the black, and Whitney was so busy taking calls from teachers and training docents that she said she “was basically reduced to a reservationist.”

Tours and school outreaches became more specialized, with students learning about such areas as conservation, predator-prey relationships, biological and behavioral adaptations, and reproduction. Programs were also tailored to specific age groups, with emphasis on reaching children at their intellectual level without talking down to them. As well, Whitney worked closely with schools and teachers to make certain that the zoo’s programs fit the schools’ curriculum.

Much of the focus of teaching has been, admittedly, on younger zoo visitors. A child’s enthusiasm for animals often wanes when they reach adulthood, yet if they can be introduced to the amazing world of wildlife from an early age that will make an impression on them that will last throughout their lives.

Adults can become quite interested in education at the zoo, as well. However, as Whitney pointed out, the message is often conveyed to them indirectly. “That’s why you practice the ‘trickle up’ theory,” said Whitney. “We have a trickle up theory when we’re teaching kids. It’s amazing how much parents will learn from their kids after they have an experience at the zoo. I’ll never forget all the parents that would come up to me and tell me at the end of the day of summer camp—and we only did half-day camps. The kids were only there three

A docent stops to tell visitors about the mandrill exhibit during an education tour (photo courtesy Potter Park Zoo Society).

hours—and the parents would say to me, 'Well, you know, I don't get that they're learning anything.' And I tried to tell them to be patient; that we cover a lot of material during our camp; and I said that at the end of a camp they're just emotionally and mentally exhausted.... Every year [after the Members Picnic, which was also after camp] the parents would come to me and say that, during the walk around the zoo with their kids, all this stuff just comes pouring forth on what the kids have learned about the animals during camp but were unable to verbalize.... Parents of the four and five year olds were amazed at how much [they] remembered. They become their own little tour guide as they go around the zoo" and teach their parents about the animals.

Because of the way children learn, it is important that they get firsthand experience when learning about wildlife. Children are tactile learners, which means that when they are able to physically touch something, or get their hands involved in some other way, they retain what they've learned better. This is one aspect of education in which Potter Park Zoo particularly excels. Some zoos, such as the Detroit Zoo, do not allow their docents to handle any of the animals. At Potter Park, however, docents are trained to work with some of the animals hands-on (though always with unthreatening, nonvenomous, and smaller animals, such as rabbits, ferrets, turtles, and various birds, insects, and reptiles). As a docent myself, I can tell you from personal experience that nothing excites children more about an animal than being able to reach out and touch its fur, or scales, a feather, or even a hard shell. That connection makes the animal come alive for them. In fact, there have been a number of occasions during a program when a boy or girl has asked me whether the animal I am holding is "real" or "alive." When I show them that it is and that they can experience it close up, they are amazed and full of wonder and excitement. In an age where television, computers, and video games substitute for reality, such experiences are indispensable for youngsters who need to gain a genuine appreciation of nature.

As well as touching the animals, kids are able to participate in many hands-on projects at Potter Park Zoo. At ZooKambi and the Big Zoo Lesson, they have the opportunity to make enrichment treats for the animals, conduct projects that mimic real scientific experiments, or survey animals' behaviors, analyze them, and come to their own conclusions. Such adventures last much longer in a child's mind than information learned from reading a textbook.

Parent participation is valuable as well, noted Dennis Laidler, the zoo's current education curator. Referring to the Big Zoo Lesson, he

Teachers from all around Michigan volunteer to be trained to teach kids for the successful Big Zoo Lesson, created by 2000 Michigan Teacher of the Year Margaret Holtschlag. Zoo Education Curator Dennis Laidler (seated far right) organizes the annual program (photo courtesy Potter Park Zoo Society).

said "parent participation is a part of that model. It's amazing the feedback you get from parents. They learn so much while they're here, and that is important on several different [levels]. One, we know that students learn better when parents participate in education, period. And two, parents are the role models for their children, and when they continue to learn as adults that also sends a message—a very important message, not only about lifelong learning, but how important questioning things is, always reading and asking questions."[5]

Education Program Participation (2005)*

In 2005 the Potter Park Zoo Society ran 354 individual education programs (tours, school outreaches, etc.) attended by 20,111 students. Of these programs, 243 (about 69%) were scheduled by groups outside of Lansing and were attended by 15,835 people (79% of the total). The figures below do not include students who attended The Big Zoo Lesson (980 participating students) or ZooKambi (the zoo's summer camp, for which figures were not available, but the numbers run into the hundreds); nor does the table below include the thousands who attended animal demonstrations and other educational programs as part of one of the zoo's many other special events, such as Wonderland of Lights and the monthly Wonders of the Wild free lecture series. If all of these events are factored in as well, Education Curator Dennis Laidler estimated that between 35,000 and 40,000 people gain from an educational experience at Potter Park Zoo every year.

Origin	Number of Students
Lansing	4,276
Ingham County (excluding Lansing)	5,709
Eaton County	1,687
Clinton County	620
All Other Michigan Counties	7,819
TOTAL	20,111

*Source: Potter Park Zoo Society

EXCEEDING EXPECTATIONS

Whitney left Potter Park Zoo at the end of 1999 to take a job as head of education at the Jacksonville Zoo in Florida. After ten years,

When children are able to see—and even touch—real animals, the experience leaves a much more tangible impression on them than simply watching a program on television. Potter Park Zoo's education programs are therefore a crucial means of passing along an appreciation of nature to the next generation (photo courtesy Potter Park Zoo Society).

she had established a smooth-running program that was mostly maintained by docents, so the transition to a new education curator went quite smoothly. The choice for the opening was Dennis Laidler. With a B.S. in fish and wildlife biology from Lake Superior State and a master's degree from Michigan State University, Laidler also possessed extensive experience as both a biologist and an educator. His résumé includes work with the U.S. Forest Service, where among other things he worked as education coordinator for the youth program, as a naturalist in Lapeer County, at a wildlife center in Oregon called Wildlife Images (where he became knowledgeable in handling raptors and traveled the country as a teacher), and as an educator for Michigan United Conservation Clubs, which also involved considerable travel.

With his hard science education and teaching background, Laidler was an ideal hire for Potter Park Zoo's education department. Although Whitney had created a quality program for the zoo, Laidler, who was hired in May 2000, jumped in and expanded it even more. It was good timing, since construction on the new Education Center, which Whitney had helped to design before she left, was just being

Education Curator Dennis Laidler is especially fond of raptors, but has an extensive all-around background in wildlife education (photo by Jim Fordyce).

completed that summer. The building, which was part of the new complex of structures at the front of the zoo, included quarters for all the education animals, plus two classrooms and a library/media center. It made for a solid base of operations for the education department.

In addition to taking over the ZooKambi summer courses, a brand new program practically jumped into Laidler's lap. Margaret Holtschlag, who had been named Michigan Teacher of the Year in 2000, approached Laidler with the idea for The Big Zoo Lesson. Together, they created the program in which area teachers are first trained in wildlife education and then bring their classes to the zoo to receive a weeklong course all about animals. It is the first program of its type in the United States and has been incredibly successful every year, with teachers practically fighting for the chance to fill one of the forty or so available slots. In fact, The Big Zoo Lesson has become so popular that the former outdoor classroom by the duck pond had to be remodeled so that there would be three classrooms available for students.

More recently, Laidler has worked with Dr. Tara Harrison to create VEZU—"Veterinarians, Education, Zoos, and yoU"—in which docents, vet students, and practicing veterinarians visit students and tell them about veterinary medicine. Depending on the grade level, VEZU, which is now in full swing after the pilot program proved to be a success in the spring of 2006, teaches young people about the profession of being a vet, or how to choose the best vet for your pet's needs, or, for older students, how to not only become a vet but how to also run a vet practice, including all the business elements involved. Laidler expanded the program further in 2007.

Looking to the future, technology is going to be taking a larger and larger role in education at Potter Park Zoo. Dwindling budgets in the economically depressed mid-Michigan region has led many schools to limit or completely suspend field trips to the zoo. Because of this, the outreach program is becoming increasingly important, but Laidler is also fostering another solution: distance learning. Currently, the zoo is using two-way video conferencing, combined with video clips, to bring its programs into the classroom. This way, live discussions can take place, as well as presenting clips to illustrate various animals and their behaviors. Such programs can obviously be transmitted throughout Michigan and the United States.

"There are things we can show with a virtual field trip that we can't show on site," Laidler remarked. "Now, I want to make clear that we never want to replace an on-site visit with a virtual field trip. Meeting and interacting with the animals up close is the ideal way." Yet, if a school class can't make it to the zoo because there's no money, it's the best alternative and one the zoo is lucky to be able to offer.

In the near future, educators and students may be able to participate in Potter Park education programs offered through interactive Web sites and even podcasts, Laidler revealed. In addition, he is hoping to work more closely with surrounding education centers, including MSU, Lansing Community College, and the Impression Five Science Museum in downtown Lansing to create classes that combine what these institutions have to offer along with the zoo's expertise and resources.

College Students at Potter Park Zoo

While most people think of Potter Park Zoo as a place for young children to learn, Lansing's zoo has also served as a useful educational resource for college students for many years. Currently, Dr. Tara Harrison estimates that Dr. Jim Sikarskie at Michigan State University has about twenty-five to thirty veterinary students in his class that use the zoo as a resource, and she herself teaches about ten to twelve. Anywhere between three to ten students also observe Dr. Harrison each time she performs a medical procedure, and she completes at least two major ones each month. She teaches about 150 to 200 students each year, including veterinary students from Michigan State University and vet tech students from both MSU and Baker College. To summarize:

- Over sixty vet tech students from Baker College in Jackson, Michigan, learn about zoo and exotic animal medicine at Potter Park each year.
- Over 250 MSU vet and vet tech students either study animal medicine or learn about at least one zoo animal case at Potter Park Zoo every year.
- Dr. Harrison works with at least eight zoo keeper interns each year.
- At least 200 students from MSU use the zoo as a research for taking a course or for teaching each year.
- Zoo employees lecture to 200 to 300 or more students each year at MSU.

THE HOPE FOR WILDLIFE LIES WITH PEOPLE

Human beings are the reason wildlife is disappearing around the globe. That's the bad news. The good news is that people still have a chance to save it. For that to happen, attitudes need to change profoundly, and that, simply put, is why education is now a core value at Potter Park and all zoos all over the world.

"The biggest part of wildlife management," explained Laidler, "(and it took a while for me to understand this, too) isn't managing the species or even the habitat, it's people management. By that I mean, educating the public so that they understand why certain management policies need to be implemented. In some cases it is a government agency, sometimes it has to be legislated.... In things like ... pollution, which affects every part of our planet, the only way you can make a difference is by individuals not only understanding what the problems are and what they can do, but it isn't a complete job of education unless you change attitudes and behavior. Just getting [people] interested and concerned isn't enough. It's the first step, but basically you gain interest and they acquire knowledge, then hopefully they have a change in attitude, which leads to a change in behavior."

One of the challenges of changing poor attitudes toward nature and wildlife, remarked Laidler, is that human beings are notorious for their desire for instant gratification. If they participate in a conservation effort of some kind, they want to see quick results to feel as if they have accomplished something. However, nature is not that cooperative. It can take decades, even generations, for a habitat or a species to recover once it has been compromised or destroyed by human actions. This can cause those who are not already dedicated scientists or other wildlife professionals to lose interest and enthusiasm.

This is perhaps why, of the zoo's four missions, Kelliann Whitney commented, "Believe it or not, I think recreation is first and foremost. Zoos have to provide a safe, inviting environment that is an outdoor experience. An opportunity for people to reconnect with nature. And I think once you get them there and get them sold on that aspect, then I think education is next. Gerald Durrell in [the movie documentary] *The Keepers of Eden* I think put it very succinctly in that zoos are living libraries for their communities. Most people in a community are never going to have the opportunity to go and see these animals in the wild, and in some cases with endangered species will never have the opportunity to experience that. So a zoo becomes a living museum ... and gives everyone an opportunity to glimpse the world outside of their community. Education has to be first and foremost one of the strongest parts for justifying the existence of zoos today. Without education you can't really have effective conservation. If people don't understand the issues that are facing wildlife and habitats and also the local people who live in and around those habitats that are being destroyed, then you can't cultivate that next level of caring to promote conservation and find support for conservation programs."

The current executive director of the Zoo Society, Diane McNeil, feels that conservation and education are inextricably linked missions for any zoo. "We are the only ones who can talk for these animals," she said, "so we're the only ones who can tell their story, whether it's good, bad, or ugly. I think it's our duty to [convey] the importance of their role on earth to the people."[6]

10

Challenges of the 21st Century

By the 1990s, everyone at Potter Park Zoo could deservedly give themselves a big pat on the back for what they had accomplished over the last quarter century. The animal collection, thanks in large part to Gerry Brady, had been greatly diversified and now included an array of rare and endangered species in the SSP program; education programs, supported by the Society and its growing cadre of docents (63 active docents by 1998, and 117 by 2008) and other volunteers, were serving over 35,000 students—young and old—annually; and by 2000, with the addition of Dr. Harrison to the full-time staff, medical science and research was reaching a level that any respectable zoo would be proud of.

But with such successes came a pressure to grow, to build new exhibits, to raise more money to support the animals, staff, buildings, and operating expenditures, and to meet the increasingly strict standards of quality set by the AZA. Regarding the latter, each time Potter Park Zoo had been inspected and accredited by the AZA—in 1986, 1991, 1996, and 2001—it had done so conditionally (the zoo was last fully accredited in 2002, and so the next full inspection was moved to 2007). This meant going back and correcting any problems within one year of being inspected. Conditional accreditation is not unusual for a small zoo, and according to Eric Reickel, the Lansing Department of Parks and Recreation Director from 1989 to 2000, about half of the country's small- and medium-sized zoos have to correct certain problems after an AZA inspection. A chronic lack at the Lansing zoo for AZA standards had been the fact that Potter Park did not have a full-time curator under Gerry Brady. This condition was filled when Dr. Harrison took over both veterinary and general curatorial duties for the zoo. The AZA inspection for 2007 had its own unique worries, and they centered largely on money.

MONEY REMAINS TIGHT

The financial situation at Potter Park Zoo had been eased somewhat in 1991, after Carol Webster and the Society's board of directors, with the full support of Eric Reickel, went before the City Council and convinced them to put a new millage on the ballot that would earmark funds for capital improvements to the zoo, as well as the parks system. The millage, which replaced the funds lost by the zoo when the 1986 bond issue had matured, passed easily by the supportive Lansing voters, who have continued to renew it ever since. Councilman Sid Worthington was one of the first to support it, hoping that money would go to the golf courses, and he rallied support from others in the Council. Reickel characterized the millage as "the savior to the whole park system."[1]

As early as 1990, the City was considering other options for the zoo's financial future, including regionalization—having one or more counties support the zoo with their tax dollars instead of just Lansing—and turning over management of Potter Park Zoo to the Society. The notion was instigated by the fact that Lansing's budget was in a crunch due to a mild recession at the time, which also inspired Mayor Terry McKane to suggest that $750,000 from the millage be used to run the zoo. However, as *Lansing State Journal* reporter Tim Makinen explained in an article at the time, "The millage question presented to voters said money would pay for capital improvements at the zoo.... Zoo facilities would be neglected and residents misled if the millage is used for daily operations, [Carol] Webster said."[2]

The debate on how the zoo was to be run and by whom would then be set aside, but it would be raised repeatedly over the coming years until it reached a head in 2006. But before we get ahead of ourselves, there were other things going on at Potter Park Zoo other than money problems.

MORE IMPROVEMENTS, NEW ARRIVALS

With the 1991 parks millage passed by Lansing residents, the financial base for the zoo was fairly secure, but it was still not enough to support the addition of any major projects. After the completion of the 1989 renovation of the Feline/Primate House, the next big expense had been refurbishing the old elephant building to accommodate the black rhinos. In 1992, the barnyard area underwent a complete revamp at a cost of just under $400,000, including renovating the barn and adding a large trellis over the walkway that runs the length of the yard. As Reickel recalled, during his decade there in the 1990s "we improved the camel exhibit," added the gazebo in 1994, and almost all the other structures, walkways, and exhibits were worked on in one way or another. "In my mind there's nothing in that zoo that did not change, with the exception of the Feline/Primate House," during the '90s.

The money for these improvements came from the millage, as well as from the Society's fund-raising efforts. Probably more exciting than such necessary structural improvements, however, was that Gerry Brady's efforts to bring in breeding pairs of endangered species was already paying off in the early 1990s. A magnificent Siberian Tiger named Ivan sired three cubs with his mate, Helga, in 1992. Helga left the zoo in early 1995 for the Lee Richardson Zoo in Garden City, Kansas, where she was mated with a tiger named Big Bob and gave birth to another litter of cubs. Meanwhile, visitors to Potter Park were treated not only to the spectacle of frolicking cubs but, soon after, by the sight of a white Bengal tiger named Kitra, who came to Lansing on loan from the Henry Doorly Zoo of Omaha, Nebraska, in 1995. Other tigers have come and gone since then, including a Sumatran tiger named Tabib who arrived in 1996. Siberian—or Amur—tigers are more suited to Michigan's climate than other subspecies, so it was eventually determined that Potter Park Zoo would focus on Amurs. Ivan would become the grand old gentleman of the zoo, living a long life until his arthritis became so severe that he had to be mercifully euthanized in 2003 at the age of twenty.

Big cats have always been a mainstay at Potter Park Zoo. In addition to the tigers, the African lions have always been popular, and in the 1990s the zoo was the home to Amboselli and Samburu, who came to Potter Park as cubs from the Gladys Porter Zoo in Brownsville, Texas, in 1989. Named after two African wildlife parks, Samburu, the male, and Amboselli, the female, were brother and sister and

African lions Samburu (right) and Amboselli were longtime residents at the zoo (photo by Constance Wardell courtesy of Potter Park Zoo Society).

very attached to one another. Because they were siblings, they were not allowed to breed (Samburu was vasectomized), though that did not seem to prevent him from trying! Samburu was a grumpy lion who did not take too kindly to his keepers, always determined to show them who was boss. The powerful beast would also put on a show for visitors, attacking the thick glass of his exhibit when guests came by, standing on his hind legs and showing the humans that he was indeed the king! When he contracted cancer at an advanced age, the bond he shared with his sister was clear. For many days Samburu had to be isolated from Amboselli as he underwent chemotherapy treatments; Amboselli could hear him below the building, and would hover by the door for days, awaiting his return.

In 1998, an extraordinary and highly endangered cat, the snow leopard, became a success story when the female gave birth to two cubs: a male and a female. The cubs would be favorites at the zoo for several years, especially Little Girl, who had the endearing habit of holding her long tail in her mouth as if she were sucking on a security blanket.

> "In the end, we will conserve only what we love. We will love only what we understand. We will understand what we are taught."
>
> —Baba Dioum
> Conservationist from Senegal

Another accomplishment came in 2007 when a scimitar-horned oryx, a species extinct in the wild, was born at Potter Park. The zoo had also been having some success with red pandas, also known as lesser pandas, which had been brought to Lansing in the late 1990s.

The hopes for breeding the zoo's black rhinos, Jimma and Rafiki (aka Ebony), were much more problematic, however. Jimma,

Jimma and Ebony in 1997 (photo courtesy Mary Anne McNamara).

although he was a very sweet rhinoceros whom the keepers adored, fell a bit short in the love department. Although he appeared to be attracted to Rafiki, he never seemed to grasp how all the anatomy was supposed to work and did not successfully mate with his lovely partner.

Thus it was that, with profound regret, Jimma departed Potter Park in 2005 for the Cleveland Zoo and was replaced by a male named Spike from the same Ohio zoo. How does one move a two-ton rhino? One step at a time. Because using anesthesia to put the rhino to sleep for the move was not the best option—too dangerous—keepers trained Jimma over many months to become accustomed to a one-ton rhino-safe crate. Once Jimma was used to the crate and knew that going inside would not hurt him, he was very cooperative about entering it himself and was safely trucked to Cleveland.

Spike was quite taken by Rafiki, and it was hoped they would mate successfully. Rhinos have an eighteen-month gestation period, so the zoo was in for a long wait, even if they did mate. Sometimes, the fruits of the zoo's labors require considerable time and much patience, but with fewer than 2,000 black rhinos left in the wild today, it is worth the wait.

Unfortunately, bad luck plagued Potter Park Zoo when it came to black rhinos. Ebony developed serious foot infections in 2007 and had to undergo months of treatment, including toe amputations. Then, shockingly, on February 8, 2008, Spike was found dead in his exhibit. The culprit was renal failure. Gerry Brady expressed the staff's confusion over the sudden tragedy: "He was fantastic.... He was eating and behaving normally, just your typically healthy rhino.... Spike was so special to us and close to our hearts. There are so many people out in the community that loved the rhino. It's going to take a while to get over the grieving process."[3]

The second of a one-two punch came on April 6, when Ebony died. Ebony's problems had developed into a life-threatening blood disease commonly called "black rhino syndrome." This disease, which has become fairly common in zoos, resulted in a series of health problems that conspired to end her life, including pneumonia; gastric and dermal ulcers; fluid in her uterus, chest, and abdomen; anemia; and foot infections. The staff managed to save Ebony's ovaries, however, and they were flown to the Cincinnati Zoo, where eighteen eggs were harvested for fertilization research.

Because of what can only be called a poor record in keeping healthy, breeding black rhinos at Potter Park Zoo, the staff has been seriously considering replacing black rhinos with white rhinos, which have had a better record at North American zoos of remaining healthy. While not quite as rare as the black rhino, white rhinos are still in serious decline in Africa.

While the zoo staff hoped for success with the rhinos, there was great news on March 26, 2005, when Kendra the Amur tiger gave birth to four cubs sired by Charlie. Although one of the cubs succumbed to the calicivirus, one male and two female cubs survived and have been thriving at the zoo ever since. Both adult tigers were on loan from other zoos (Kendra from St. Louis and Charlie from the Beardsley Zoo), and when the cubs got a little bigger, the older cats left Potter Park to make room for the growing cubs. Tigers become mature at about two years of age, so at least two of the three cubs will have to be moved soon. As of spring 2008, however, they were all still at the zoo, with the sisters being kept separate from their brother. Depending on the needs of the SSP, they may or may not be matched up with mates at other zoos.

It seems that with each passing year, Potter Park Zoo has been achieving greater success with animal births. In 2006, for example, the zoo saw the birth of a Bactrian camel (the fourth to be born there), a cotton-top tamarin monkey, a mongoose lemur, and a Magellanic

The zoo—and, indeed, the entire community—was thrilled to see three Amur tiger cubs successfully born to Charlie and Kendra (photo by Bruce Bolender courtesy of the Potter Park Zoo Society).

penguin. The extremely endangered Bali mynah birds also exhibit mating behavior and laid some eggs, though none have hatched at the time of this writing.

Because Potter Park Zoo brought in a lot of animals in the 1980s when Gerry Brady first arrived and began his efforts at obtaining a greater variety of species, by the 2000s many of the residents at the zoo had become quite geriatric. That is all part of the natural cycle of life, however, and younger animals were already arriving in 2005 and 2006, including two new otters and three arctic fox for the North American exhibit.

NEW ENTRANCE COMPLEX AND EDUCATION CENTER

In 1995 there was also cause for celebration when Potter Park Zoo marked its seventy-fifth anniversary. The zoo organized events for the public and there was much reflection on its past and future. A few years later, in 1999, a poll conducted by the *Lansing State Journal* listed Potter Park Zoo as mid-Michigan's most popular attraction and also the best family attraction. Good news, and reason enough for the zoo to plan one of its most ambitious projects ever.

The new entry complex, including the education building, gift shop, and administrative offices, opened in 2000 (photo by Kevin Hile).

The zoo and Society had long operated using less than ideal offices for its administrative and educational uses. The zoo administration and keepers worked out of converted space in the former Dog House, the oldest building at the zoo; there was also an office beneath the Bird/Reptile House, and the historic Scott House in downtown Lansing was used by the Society director and for docent meetings. In addition, classes for kids were held in the converted pond overlook building, which lacked a bathroom and running water. Although some felt that additional fund-raising efforts should go to new exhibits, with so much going on it was also important to have a base of operations to manage it all. Furthermore, it was felt that an updated entrance and gift store was needed for the public. As Eric Reickel noted, "A first impression is a lasting impression, and that's why I did not like the entrance to the zoo. Some people said, well, you could put three million dollars more into the zoo and not done that beautiful entrance that you have, but Carol [Webster] needed the entrance for the concessions and the souvenir stand.... And then we needed an interpretive center and offices for the Zoo Society, as well as the director. We were operating out of some little one-horse building."

In addition to the Zoovenir shop, concessions stand, ticket booths, and administration offices, the highlight of the planned new entrance complex was the 10,400 square foot Exploration and Discovery Center for Education. This building would contain offices for the education curator, docents, concessions manager, and special events manager, as well as a media center/library, a welcome center, a large conference room, two classrooms, a fully equipped kitchen, quarters for all the small animals used in education programs, and the special exhibits room that now houses the Coral Reef Exhibit.

As had become a matter of tradition for Potter Park Zoo, raising the approximately $3 million for the ambitious project (half of which was for the education center alone) was the challenge. Negotiating with the City, Carol Webster and Eric Reickel hammered out an agreement in which it was resolved that Lansing would match what the Society raised through private donations and other fund-raising efforts. To help out, even Ivan the tiger got into the act: tiles were made including his massive paw print signature, with sales going toward the new buildings' construction.

Webster hoped that a huge chunk of the $1.6 million the Society wanted to raise could come from land donated to the City by the Priggooris family. The Priggoorises owned a large tract of property outside the city limits that they wished to donate as parkland. However, because it was outside of Lansing, the City planned to sell the property and use the $400,000 from the sale for the parks department. Half the land was sold to former MSU president and head of the Michigan Department of Natural Resources Gordon Geier and his partner, Dennis Fijalkowski, who built a headquarters for a nonprofit nature organization; the other half was sold to the local Eyde family. "I tried to get that as a donation from the Priggoorises to the Zoo Society," said Reickel. "Well, the Council says, 'No, this is our property. We sold it.' But the Council did honor Mr. Priggooris's request to associate his name to whatever the funds went into." Thus, the money went into the education center, which is now officially named after Angel Priggooris.

The opening of the new entrance complex in the summer of 2000, at a final cost of $3.3 million, was a proud moment for the zoo, making that strong first impression that Reickel wanted visitors to have as they entered the wildlife park. The education center also provided the Society with fund-raising opportunities not only by providing more space for classes but also through rental fees from the large Safari Room conference area.

To make the Safari Room even more profitable, Webster wanted to have the option for guests to serve alcohol at their private parties; this

Docent Sue Merritt teaches kids about a snow leopard skeleton in the zoo's education building (photo courtesy Potter Park Zoo Society).

would make the room even easier to rent out. The City Council, however, denied the Society an alcohol license. As one of the zoo's volunteers, Karlene Rabidoux, pointed out in a letter to the *Lansing State Journal*'s editor, "Such a request is not entirely without precedent in this city.... The Zoo Society is asking for nothing more than to be included in an existing ordinance permitting beer and wine service within the grounds of the Turner-Dodge House, Scott House and Park, and Cooley Gardens."[4] Alcohol is also permitted at the Impression Five Museum, Rabidoux further stated. Yet the City Council felt that the zoo was too family-oriented (as opposed to the science museum?) to allow alcohol, even though other zoos, such as the Detroit Zoo and John Ball Zoo, also permit it for private functions. "I look at the zoo as being a place that's primarily for kids," argued City Councilman Lou Adado, Jr. "Our society has done a real good job the last several years cautioning kids against alcohol use and I don't think the two go together. It would be an inconsistent message."[5] Despite that assertion, since that time restrictions have been eased and the zoo is allowed to serve beer and wine on special occasions, if not on a regular basis.

A NEW MASTER PLAN, A NEW CENTURY

Years after the zoo had paid architects to devise the first master plan in 1984, it had become clear that Potter Park was not heading in precisely the same direction as had been originally envisioned. So, in 1995, Reickel, Brady, Webster, Lansing Mayor David Hollister, and the City Council got together and hired McFadzean Everly Associates in Evanston, Illinois, to help Potter Park develop a brand new Master Plan. Again, the idea was to refocus efforts on the direction in which the zoo wished to go.

One of the fundamental concepts underlying the new plan was to reorganize the exhibits in a way that was reflective of what other zoos were doing; that is, to group animal species according to the regions of the world from which they originated. Thus, there would be a South American area, an Arctic/Sub-Arctic area, an African Theme area, and so on. Such a plan would not only give visitors a feeling of embarking on a safari throughout the world as they walked the grounds, but also might facilitate education by having the animals grouped in a more logical manner. Furthermore, the plan called for a section of the zoo—the pond and gardens area—to be designated as the Red Cedar Ecological Exhibit.

As with the original Master Plan, this new plan was also ambitious, calling for state-of-the-art exhibits that both mimicked natural habitat and offered visitors unique viewing opportunities, such as observation areas below ground where swimming seals and fish could be viewed through glass. The plan also called for new animals, such as polar bears, moose, caribou, seals, giraffes, zebras, duikers, jackals, cheetahs, Japanese macaques, crocodiles, and even Komodo dragons. (Adding polar bears at Potter Park Zoo is now unlikely, since Detroit and Toledo both have outstanding polar bear exhibits already; also, Japanese macaques will probably never be seen at Lansing's zoo, because there is too much potential for them to be carrying diseases.) Finally, as if that were not enough, a tram ride was also specified in the plan.

Of course, this would all cost many millions of dollars. Realizing the little zoo and cash-strapped city could ill afford to realize their dream all at once, the construction was divided into eight phases, each costing between $1.5 and $2.5 million, for a total estimated expense of $16,262,500. The new Master Plan also predicted that regionalizing the zoo would be a likely strategy to fund the many improvements envisioned.

Just a couple of years after this new Master Plan was completed, Potter Park Zoo appeared to be struggling yet again. As it entered the twenty-first century, Lansing's zoo had already experienced some hardships. From 1998 to 2001, summer attendance had been slowly declining. Some blamed this on unusually hot summer weather, while others noted that downtown Lansing and East Lansing were beginning to offer some other public events that were drawing away visitors, such as the Common Grounds music festival and the East Lansing Aquatic Center that had recently opened. In addition, nearby zoos were increasingly in competition with Potter Park. The Detroit Zoo opened its stunning Ring of Life Arctic exhibit in 2001; the Binder Park Zoo had a sprawling new African savannah exhibit where animals such as giraffe wandered freely over acres of grassy, rolling fields; even little John Ball Zoo had a state-of-the-art tide pool exhibit that was impressive. Entertainment opportunities were becoming more competitive in Michigan, a fact that did not go unrecognized by the zoo and the Society.

A temporary blow to the zoo's image also came unwelcomed on June 23, 2001, when the estranged wife of a state police detective was shot to death on the path leading up to the zoo gates. Shockingly, she was shot not only in the daytime, but also in front of her five-year-old daughter. While many area residents strongly suspected the detective, a skilled sharp-shooter whose wife was leaving him and who had confessed to accessing a police database just before the killing to research her activities and acquaintances, he was never charged with the murder, which remains unsolved to this day. Although the killing, like the one back in 1980, was not actually on zoo grounds, the crime was bad publicity and likely dissuaded some people from visiting the park at least for a while, especially when *Lansing State Journal* headlines unhelpfully referred to it in its coverage as the "zoo shooting."

Potter Park Zoo had been showing great progress, but was it enough to survive in the new millennium? To add to its worries, a new mayor in Lansing was about to target the zoo for budget cuts.

ZOO FUNDING: WHAT IS THE ANSWER?

As with the original master plan, the new vision for Potter Park Zoo was at risk of never being fulfilled if financial problems continued to plague the little Lansing zoo. The debate about regionalization, which had percolated in the background for about fifteen years, came to a head in 2006. Lansing had a new mayor, Virg Bernero, who had defeated incumbent Tony Benavides and was on a mission to streamline the city budget, which was operating $11 million in the red due to the sluggish economy and skyrocketing expenses. In addition to cuts across the board, Bernero wanted to reduce the zoo's budget, eliminating two zoo keepers from the permanent staff.

If such a plan were carried out, everyone at the zoo knew, there would not be enough people to care for the over 400 animals that were in the park. This would set off a domino effect: without enough keepers, the zoo could not take care of its animal collection properly; the AZA would recognize this and probably deny Potter Park its accreditation after the 2007 inspection; without accreditation, all the zoo's SSP animals would have to find other homes and Potter Park Zoo would be reduced to little more than a roadside attraction. Gone would be such animals as the tigers, snow leopards, mandrills, lemurs, tamarin monkeys, wolves, oryxes, and much more.

Should such a worse-case scenario occur, Diane McNeil, who was hired as the Society's executive director when Carol Webster retired

Dear Mayor Bernero,

Did you go to the Potter Park Zoo? Because I did. My class went to the Big Zoo Lesson in February and we learned so much. It was good for my brain. We were there for five days, and we know what it's about. We drew pictures and wrote observations about what they were doing. The baby lion tamarinds were so cute and we studied them a lot.

I don't want the Potter Park Zoo to lose money. The Potter Park Zoo means a lot to me. If we can't have the money, no one will have fun. It is fun there on Christmas, Halloween, and all of that stuff.

I love the Potter Park Zoo. There are many good things about Potter Park Zoo. We went to see the baby tigers playing and growing. I saw the red panda, and the snow leopard chasing its tail. The mother lioness was pawing on the glass. The golden lion tamarind petted its paw on the window and then it yawned and I saw its teeth. It's smaller than a sticker star.

When we were making the wolves' some food, it was out of meat, fish and Jell-O. They were looking for it very good. They were looking behind trees, under logs, everywhere in their cage. It was fun and funny.

I went to the coral reef fishes, when I saw the fishes kissing. I knew right away why they are called kissing fishes. When we were at the coral reef, we drew our own fishes, and an anemone. When we all said, "Anemone," we laughed. It was funny.

When we were in our classroom at the zoo, we were touching snakes and turtles. I loved touching the snakes. I had never touched a snake before. It was cool. When Dr. Tara the vet came with two girls, she answered our questions about the animals that we had written on the stickies. When we went to meet Mr. Dennis, he showed us a binturong and it made tricks.

After Lansing's Mayor Virg Bernero proposed cuts to the zoo, many students from Lansing wrote touching letters asking him not to reduce the zoo's budget. Here are three of those letters—with the children's names obscured to protect their privacy (letters courtesy Potter Park Zoo Society).

I hope you get the money for the zoo. I am really worried whether Potter Park Zoo will be there. If you don't pay money, you won't have a lot of zookeepers. It is important to get the money so you can feed the animals, or they will die or get sick. They are my friends, and they feel like a family, a real family. I know they're not like people, but they're family. If you don't, we won't have all this stuff and we won't know how animals eat, get babies, and what they eat. I love the Potter Park Zoo. Everybody does. That is their best place in the whole wide world in Michigan. So please pay -- I want you to!

Sincerely,

Woodcreek Magnet School
for Math, Science and Engineering

Dear Mayor Bernero,

Do you know why I want to save Potter Park Zoo? Because the animals could get hurt. And when they are hurt, other people can't see them and enjoy the fun. It is important to me because if I get to see the animals and the others won't, I would feel it is unfair for them.

What if a class came to Potter Park Zoo and didn't see the animals, like we did? We weren't there for just one day, we were there for five whole days and I got to know the zoo very much. I learned a lot about the zoo. I learned a lot about the mongoose lemurs because that was the animal I studied about. I learned when they lick themselves they could be combing themselves or taking a bath. We got to touch a turtle and I felt its shell. It was smooth as a mirror. When I touched it, the body pulled in.

When my class was at the zoo, we made something for they wolves. How we made the wolves' food is, we had fish and meat. We cut the fish and rolled the meat up. We put it in something and when we were done, they poured Jell-O in it and put it in the refrigerator and let it freeze. When they were frozen, and took it out, they fed it to the wolves. The wolves used their noses to find the food.

The zoo needs money because if there is not enough zookeepers, the animals won't get fed in time and they might get sick. I want to go to the zoo again, so please keep giving the zoo funding.

Sincerely,

Woodcreek Magnet School
for Math, Science and Engineering

Dear Mayor Bernero,

Have you ever been to Potter Park Zoo in Lansing?! The zoo is really fun to go there. I like the zoo. You should go there some time. If you have kids, you could take them, or your wife and family. You will enjoy it. I bet they will like it too. If you don't believe me, you should ask someone who has been there. We went to the Big Zoo Lesson. We went for five whole days. We learned so much about animals.

You get to see lots of things -- lions, tigers, mongoose lemurs, golden lion tamarinds, rhinos, penguins, fish, snakes, birds, too, and owls. There are a lot of animals at Potter Park Zoo. I loved the lioness. She is so beautiful. She was pawing on the glass. The lioness liked to sleep. The male tiger's name was Charlie. He has three kids of his own. They are much fun. The lizard has a blue tongue! There are cute fish and they have "Finding Nemo" fish. I liked the kissing fish. They have a lot of snakes, birds, owls, fish and parrots. They're all different colors and they are pretty.

Why would you want to take away the zoo's money? It isn't fair. Do you know there are a lot of people that like the zoo? There are over 200 people who like the zoo. If you take away the zoo, we won't have the zoo. I don't want the animals to go back into the wild. The zoo animals are our friends. It is so much fun. Please come visit us and give the zoo more money. Please don't cut the funding. Please don't make mistakes like others. I want to keep the zoo. Please don't do that to the zoo, Mayor Bernero.

Sincerely,

Woodcreek Magnet School

in 2005, said: "Well, then we deal with that. We will just go on. You will have a smaller zoo; we will keep absolutely everything we can, and we will probably have to work it out with AZA. We could possibly be accredited [with fewer animals]…. And it will just be a giant leap backwards, and it will be something we strive to go on for again. We will ask for bigger dollars, bigger donations, and we will just go through the same darn process every year."[6]

Potter Park Zoo, despite being the oldest operating zoo in Michigan, had long been the state's poor stepchild among zoological parks. The reason for this has largely to do with location. The zoos in Detroit, Grand Rapids, and Battle Creek are surrounded by successful businesses with statewide or national prominence. In Lansing, however, the main area employers are limited to state government, Michigan State University in East Lansing, and Sparrow and Ingham Hospitals, all of which are nonprofit enterprises that are constantly seeking funds just like Potter Park Zoo; they aren't looking to donate money for tax—or more noble—purposes. The biggest corporation near the zoo is General Motors, whose largest gift to the zoo up until 2000, according to Eric Reickel, was $50,000. Not that this money was not appreciated, because it certainly was, but so many other charities approach GM for help every year that the zoo has only managed to obtain a small slice of the pie. In recent years, too, GM has had its own financial problems that have made donations less likely.

More prominent zoos in Michigan also have had the benefit of state support. A perfect example of this came in 2005, when the City of Detroit threatened to close the Detroit Zoo, explaining that it could not afford to run it any more. This shocking news was followed by a public outcry to support the zoo and keep the world-class facility open. The Detroit Zoological Society agreed to take over operations from the city, but they were able to do so largely because Governor Jennifer Granholm agreed to support the Detroit Zoo with $4 million. Potter Park has never been able to count on such largesse from state coffers because it lacks Detroit's high profile.

With a scarcity of philanthropic backing opportunities outside of city government, Society Executive Director Diane McNeil was naturally concerned when Mayor Bernero not only suggested trimming staff but also wanted to turn control of the zoo over to the Society. True, the Society had done well in raising funds for capital improvements, but if the organization had to run the zoo by itself there would barely be enough for regular operating expenses alone, meaning there would be nothing left for exhibits and other improvements.

Where Does the Money Go?

It's a typical misconception among many zoo visitors that a zoo can be supported by admissions and parking fees alone. "Why," people ask, "do I need to pay tax dollars for the zoo when they already charge me to come inside and to park?" The truth is, Potter Park Zoo costs over $2 million a year to operate, and only about $500,000 of that comes from tickets and parking. Furthermore, not all of the money that the zoo collected while the City of Lansing ran it went back to the zoo. Here's how operational income worked through the budget year of 2006 at Potter Park:

Income Source	Goes Directly To	Distribution
Admissions Fees	The City	After the fees go into the City's budget, the City determines how much goes to the zoo for operations expenses.
Millage Income*	The City	This used to go to the zoo, but according to sources at the zoo, Potter Park did not receive money from the millage for several years. This money was originally intended for zoo capital improvements.
Parking Fees	The City	None of this money has come back to the zoo for several years
Society Membership Dues	Zoo Society	Pays for education programs
Private Donations	Zoo Society	Donors usually indicate how they wish their donations to be spent. The Society honors these requests
Government Grants	Zoo Society	Education programs and capital improvements
Education Program Fees, Concessions, Animal Rides, and Special Event Fees	Zoo Society	Education programs and capital improvements

*Refers to the 1991 millage, not the 2006 millage.

McNeil made her case to the mayor and the City Council, and zoo staff and volunteers attended City Council meetings regularly to make their pleas heard. Thankfully, they were listened to, and when a new city budget was worked out, it still included full funding of staff salaries at the zoo. However, the City responded by increasing parking and admissions fees to the zoo, so that in 2006 they were approaching the same prices as those of the much larger Detroit Zoo. This was not a pleasing development for anyone at the zoo; everyone wanted Potter Park Zoo to remain an entertaining and educational experience that anyone could easily afford. In addition, the mayor proposed dipping into the millage fund intended for capital improvements to pay for salaries, something that had been tried once before in 1990. This would have meant no money for capital improvements.[7]

The good news, however, was that now the mayor and the Council were all backing the idea of regionalization, and they were working with Ingham County toward this end. The time for regionalization had, at last, come for certain.

Discussing the proposal with Ingham County commissioners brought some hopeful light to the picture, as there was considerable support for the idea from the county in which Lansing is located. Less certain, however, was whether residents in neighboring Clinton and Eaton Counties would wish to contribute as well. A powerful argument can be made that the residents of the tri-county area should support the zoo, instead of laying all the tax burden on Lansing. After all, the majority of zoo guests—about seventy percent—come from outside of Lansing and benefit from its recreational and educational offerings. Estimating that a county resident with a $200,000 home would pay about $100 annually to support the zoo through a millage, Eric Reickel put it this way: "What [residents outside Lansing] want to do, is they want to look in the mirror. And they should say to themselves, 'I have purchased a very expensive home here.... Do I want to sustain the value of my home? Do I want to bring in businesses into my community or the area in order to create a tax base to support what I want?' Because if they don't pay ... to provide quality facilities and maintain a quality park system ... then the value of your home and the interest in living in that community, and doing business in that community, is going to decline, and the value of that house is going to decline."

A ballot issue for regionalizing the zoo went on the November 2006 ballot. Given the history of support for the zoo by area residents since the 1980s, zoo officials were hopeful that such a proposal—which McNeil suggested be called Proposal Z for Zoo—would pass, despite the weak economy. Even if it did not, however, Reickel's successor to the Lansing Parks and Recreation Director position, Murdock Jemerson, pointed out that there is yet another alternative. The Michigan Recreational Authorities Act (Public Act 321) of 2000 provides legal language that allows various political entities, including counties, townships, and cities, to partner and form recreational authorities to support various projects. Such a cooperative effort is already in existence for the River Trail, which has expanded outside the City of Lansing. Adjoining jurisdictions have expressed an interest in having the trail extend into their areas and contributing to its funding. "This is another option, I feel, that could be taken in that the City of Lansing could ask for other local units to partner, to put together a recreational authority for the zoo," said Jemerson.[8]

CORAL REEFS, RIVER OTTERS, AND ARCTIC FOXES

Admittedly, the financial woes of a small zoo can make for some dreary reading. But it does serve to highlight the zoo's accomplishments all the more, because of the amount of effort that needs to go behind each step forward. Although a cloud hung over Potter Park Zoo in 2005 and 2006, it was not anything that hadn't been seen before. The zoo had limped along, financially speaking, since the end of World War II, if not before, and it had always managed to not only survive but make gradual improvements.

The coral reef exhibit includes tropical fish aquariums and (at right) a breeding facility for clown fish. In 2008 a tide pool and touch tank were added (photo by Bruce Bolender courtesy of the Potter Park Zoo Society).

With the completion of the Exploration and Discovery Center for Education, new space was available to exhibit wildlife. Initially intended to be a rotating exhibit, a large room near the front of the building first displayed the Lake Victoria Exhibit, which included endangered cichlids from Africa's largest lake, as well as various bird, insect, mammal, and reptile species from the region. A new opportunity came a few years later, however, to create a Coral Reef Exhibit. Featuring clownfish, the orange-and-white striped species made popular by the Pixar film *Finding Nemo,* the new exhibit would include a wide variety of fish, shrimp, corals, sea urchins, and anemones, as well as a facility to actually breed clownfish. In fact, the official name of the exhibit is "Clownfish, Corals, and Conservation." Education curator Dennis Laidler worked with Preuss Animal House in Lansing to obtain animals, as well as MSU and graduate student Tracy McMullan to create what is now one of the zoo's most popular attractions. Because the Coral Reef Exhibit cost about $50,000, it was decided to make it a permanent part of the zoo and will be added on to in the future. For example, a hands-on touch tank was added in 2008 to give children the tactile experiences they so crave when learning about animals.

An Arctic fox enjoys its new enclosure in the zoo's North American exhibit (photo by Bruce Bolender courtesy of the Potter Park Zoo Society).

The new river otter exhibit opened in 2006 (photo by Kevin Hile).

The river otters love their state-of-the-art swimming pool! (photos by Jim Fordyce).

On June 29, 2006, the first phase of the new North American area of the zoo—the River Otter and Arctic Fox Exhibit—was officially opened. A state-of-the-art facility costing $1 million to construct, much of which was graciously donated by the Hal and Jean Glassen Memorial Foundation, the enclosure includes a public viewing area where visitors are able to see the otters swimming underwater. Not only has this proved a delight to zoo guests, but the superior exhibit provides a much more natural habitat for the otters, as well as the Arctic fox, than the old enclosures in the seventy-year-old moats by the Bird/Reptile House. The first major new exhibit construction project of any kind since the 1989 Feline/Primate House was remodeled, this new exhibit, along with the multi-building entrance plaza, really does bring Potter Park Zoo into the twenty-first century. But would it be a sign of what was to come, or a final swan song for a zoo about to lose its accreditation and take a big step backward?

THEY SAID, "YES!"

Area residents once more proved their love of Potter Park Zoo during the election of November 7, 2006. By a two-to-one margin, Ingham county voters overwhelmingly passed the regionalization proposal and effectively saved the zoo. The millage they approved would start at 0.46 (or about $23.00 for the average Ingham county home) and then slowly decrease over two years to 0.41 mills (or about $20.50 per household). The result: instead of a $1.7 million budget from the city that was under threat of severe cuts, the zoo could now look forward to a $3.1 million annual budget that would provide it with financial stability.

And the money was sorely needed.

The passage of the millage not only meant that Potter Park Zoo could keep its exotic species and remain a vital center for conservation and education, but buildings that had once again fallen into disrepair could be fixed, brought up to building code, and improved. Another festering problem was plumbing and sewer lines beneath the zoo: they had corroded to the point where bursting water pipes were an annual occurrence. Estimates to replace the failing system ranged around $3 million. While such infrastructure maintenance is never as thrilling as the opening of a new exhibit, it is just as vital for continued AZA accreditation for Potter Park Zoo.

Thankfully, many other projects that visitors were sure to enjoy were put in the works, as well. Zoo staff and Ingham County government representatives met almost immediately after the zoo millage passed to discuss strategy for future improvements. Among the projects planned were an expanded black rhino exhibit and the new bald eagle exhibit. The zoo passed its 2007 AZA inspection with flying colors, thanks in big part to the county's willingness to make a number of speedy repairs to the grounds and exhibits.

Meanwhile, Potter Park was enjoying some animal birth successes, as well. A new male snow leopard was brought to the zoo late in 2006 for breeding, and on May 7 the next year a male cub was born (the cub was transferred to Zoo Boise that December, where it is being paired with a female for further breeding); nine new meerkats were also acquired; and a species never seen at Potter Park Zoo—Asian felines known as Pallas' cats—would replace the loss of the fishing cats. A baby male mandrill born on December 7, 2007, to a female named Abuuka, and another camel baby born in February of 2008.

In recent years there has been a growing movement at zoos around the country toward privatization, regionalization, or, as with the Detroit Zoo, having them managed by zoo societies. As of June 2007,

Exotic Asian Pallas' cats are recent additions to the zoo's collection (photo by Bruce Bolender courtesy of the Potter Park Zoo Society).

when regionalization took full effect, Potter Park Zoo joined this trend for the future of zoos across the country. Within six months, the zoo reaped a number of benefits from the turnover, including:

- Repairs to the penguin pool, which had been leaking for no less than ten years
- Repairs to the barn roofs
- Renovations to the landscaping throughout the zoo, as well as out in Potter Park
- A new entrance sign greeting visitors
- The aging aviary was torn down, as it was no longer an exhibit that could pass AZA inspections
- A new otter pool filtration system was installed
- New security, both in the form of patrolling officers and electronic security cards at the fence gates where staff enter
- Increased number of keepers from eleven to fourteen; hired a horticulturist.
- Entrance fees were lowered for Ingham County residents
- And a new Potter Park Zoo Board, comprised of concerned Ingham County residents, was established to advise the zoo on its operations

In addition, in 2008 the zoo added a new interactive activity for visitors—a tide pool touch tank—as well as a new bald eagle exhibit next to the otters. There are also plans for a rotating exhibit that will feature a different animal species each year. To further increase interaction with the guests, during the summer months there will be regularly-scheduled docent and keeper talks throughout the zoo grounds.

But Potter Park Zoo has still only realized only a fraction of its full potential. With proper funding and the continued support of local communities, there is no reason why it can't become bigger, better, and more amazing than it already is. Just in the last nine years that I have had the privilege of sharing in the education aspects of what goes on here, I have seen incredible improvements; and, after researching and writing this book, I can appreciate how much this zoo has accomplished with so very little. I hope you can as well.

Curious about the future, I asked Zoo Society Director Diane McNeil where she would like to see Potter Park Zoo ten years from now. She responded:

> I would love to see this zoo known as an educational campus. I would love every known thing that we could possibly do in teaching to be installed in the education building.... Any feasible way we would have to teach, I would love us to be on the forefront of it ... so that we could reach twice as many kids and adults as we reach now. I would love to see us so well known that our numbers go up in all things. I would love to see people come in here to look at the gardens because they're all labeled. I would love it if everything was always up to snuff, and we didn't have to worry about the barn roof falling down! It's like, we *need* this capital improvement stuff that we're not getting. As far as any other exhibits, I wouldn't even surmise to say ..., but I would hope we would have the South American exhibit by the end of ten years, and that that is something to knock your socks off.

This and more could happen at the little zoo by the Red Cedar. Back in 1969, people in Lansing and nearby really showed that they loved their zoo when they heard Herman the Mexican Burro and Jim Hough call for help. The zoo is where it is today because of all those who responded, lending a hand, donating their free time, helping to build an exhibit, or pitching in a few dollars. Potter Park Zoo does not belong to city or county government, or the AZA, or even the dedicated staff, but to all the people of mid-Michigan who have saved it time and again, pulling it back from the brink of collapse to see it reborn.

A zoo is not about exhibits and admissions fees and political squabbles. Yes, it is certainly about the animals who live there, but they are there, too, for the real purpose of the zoo: people. The zoo is here for you to learn from, to get a look at the wonders of the natural world, and to gain an appreciation of what this planet has to offer you. I cannot convey accurately enough through the written word how I heard Jim Hough nearly overcome by his feelings when he told it to me this way:

> I am tremendously warmed and emotional about what a community is about. If I had any part in all of this, it was in communication. Once you do that, and you hit a note, everybody comes roaring in together and everybody gets it done, but when it's all over with they look at the guy whose byline was in the paper and they make too much production over that. It was a lot of things going on, all those kids who sold buttons to buy Bingo, and so it went. My God, we just had an enormous amount of.... For me it was fun, and it was good fodder for the newspaper. It was fun to have the publisher ... give a

> damn about what I was doing. He was just typical of the rest of the community. They cared.[9]

I've quoted a lot of professionals in this book about the value of Potter Park Zoo, but some of the voices we haven't heard from yet are the most important. So, I'm dedicating the last few pages here to them, to let them tell you why Potter Park Zoo matters. They care, too.

3/31/06

Dear Mr. Zollner,

Thank you for giving me the best trip of my life. I learned black rhinos are endangered. The best part was the otters were being funny. Thank you for showing me all of those cool animals.

Sincerley,
Alex

Letter courtesy Potter Park Zoo Society.

October 24 1997

Dear Keith and Sue,

Thank you for coming and sharing your animals I like the farit and the parit and the blue tung skingk. Your Friend Aaron

Letter courtesy Potter Park Zoo Society.

Letter courtesy Potter Park Zoo Society.

Dear Junis,

Thank you for bringing us on the cool big cat tour. I was absaluotly nice of you to wast your time to tech us. It was so cool when the the lions raored at us then the tiger did. I wish we could do this every day of the year and I wouldn't get bord.

Sincerely,

M. 2nd grade

Letter courtesy Potter Park Zoo Society.

Timeline

1913 .... James W. Potter proposes donating fifty-eight acres of land by the Red Cedar River to the City of Lansing

July 5, 1915.... Potter Park officially opens

1920 .... Deer and elk are moved from Moores Park to Potter Park. With the addition of two raccoons and a bear, Potter Park Zoo is established

1929 .... Bird House is constructed

1930 .... Feline/Primate House is completed

1936 .... Monkey Island is built, along with small moats area by the Bird House

1941 .... Aviary built

1946 .... Theron "Ted" Downey takes over management of the zoo

1948 .... Herman the Mexican burro arrives at Potter Park Zoo

1959 .... Arboretum founded by Carl Fenner; the zoo and arboretum would have close ties until 1980, and zoo staff would care for animals at the arboretum until 2003

1965 .... Ted Downey leaves Potter Park Zoo; Jerry Miller becomes zoo supervisor

1969 .... After an inspection by U.S. Department of Agriculture veterinarians, rumors circulate that the zoo might close; Friends of the Zoo is founded

1972 .... Bingo the elephant and Fuzz the tortoise arrive

1974 .... Ellen Lumbert, the longest-serving president of the Friends of the Zoo, takes office

1974 .... The zoo train begins operations and runs until 1986

1975 .... First Open House greets visitors; this is the precursor to the current holiday tradition of Wonderland of Lights
1975 .... A flood engulfs much of the zoo; fortunately, no animals are seriously endangered
1976 .... Butch and Sunnie the African lions are born
1979 .... Bingo passes away; Tombi the elephant comes to the zoo
1980 .... Parking fee implemented
1980 .... Reptiles added to the Bird House, which is now known as the Bird/Reptile House
1981 .... New wolf exhibit and new aviary open
1984 .... The first Master Plan is written
1984 .... Lansing voters approve a $1.5 million millage to support the zoo
1986 .... New penguin exhibit opens
1986 .... Potter Park Zoo receives AZA accreditation
1987 .... New spider monkey exhibit opens
1988 .... Jerry Miller and Bill Swix leave the zoo; Doug Finley becomes new zoo director
1989 .... Tombi leaves the zoo for Indianapolis
1989 .... Feline/Primate Building reopens after a complete renovation
1989 .... Carol Webster becomes executive director of the Zoo Society
1990 .... Mashaki the rhino arrives
1992 .... Doug Finley leaves the zoo; Gerry Brady becomes new zoo director
1992 .... Ivan the tiger sires three cubs with Helga
1998 .... Two endangered snow leopards are born
2000 .... An endangered scimitar-horned oryx is born.
2000 .... New entry plaza, including a large education center, is opened
2005 .... Charlie the tiger sires three cubs with Kendra
2005 .... Diane McNeil takes over from Carol Webster as Zoo Society executive director
2006 .... New river otter/arctic fox exhibit opens, marking the first phase of the planned North American exhibit
Nov. 7, 2006 ... Ingham County residents vote “Yes” to regionalize Potter Park Zoo

July 1, 2007.... Potter Park Zoo begins its first five-year term of operations under the Ingham County Parks Department

Nov. 17, 2007. The zoo passes AZA inspections with flying colors and is accredited for another five years.

2008 .... A tide pool touch tank and new bald eagle exhibit are opened to the public.

Notes

Chapter 1

1. Birt Darling, *City in the Forest: The Story of Lansing* (New York: Stratford House, 1950).
2. Ibid.
3. "Natural Beauty of Potter Land Is Big Surprise," *Lansing State Journal,* 19 May 1913, p. 1.
4. Justin L. Kestenbaum, *Out of the Wilderness: An Illustrated History of Greater Lansing* (Woodland Hills, CA: Windsor Publications, 1981).
5. "Picnic Crowds Defy Weather, Swarm to Park," *Lansing State Journal,* 5 July 1915, pp. 1-2.
6. Maisie Downey, interviewed by Kevin Hile, May 17, 2006. All subsequent quotes from Downey are from the same interview.
7. Karen Aldag, "Arboretum a Classroom of Nature," *Lansing State Journal,* 13 July 1969, p. 3D.
8. Thelma Harnett, "Tigress Balks at Door of New Potter Park Home," *Lansing State Journal,* 6 March 1951, p. 13.
9. "Potter Park Open Friday," *Lansing State Journal,* 29 May 1952, p. 34.

Chapter 2

1. Jim Hough, interviewed by Kevin Hile, 4 February 2006. Subsequent quotes from Hough are from this interview, unless otherwise cited.
2. Bill Swix, interviewed by Kevin Hile, 25 February 2006. Other quotes from Swix are from this interview.

3. Jerry Miller, interviewed by Kevin Hile, 21 February 2006.
4. Doug Finley, interviewed by Kevin Hile, 7 February 2006.
5. Jim Hough, *The Onlooker Looks Back: On the Best of 25 Years of Columns from the Lansing State Journal* (Lansing, MI: Kin Press, 1985).
6. Jim Hough, "Zoo Has Friends," *Lansing State Journal,* 6 February 1972, p. 4J.
7. Ellen and Sonny Lumbert, interviewed by Kevin Hile, 1 February 2006.
8. John Tear, "Zoo Shackled, Just Like Bingo: Good Intentions, but Animals Overseers at Odds," *Lansing State Journal,* 9 June 1974, pp. 1-2B.
9. Jim Hough, "Fund Drive 'For the Birds,'" *Lansing State Journal,* 13 August 1978, p. 73.
10. Jim Hough, "Lansing's Potter Park Zoo Rated Outstanding for City Our Size," *Lansing State Journal,* 15 August, 1976, p. 94.

CHAPTER 3

1. Jim Hough, interviewed by Kevin Hile, 4 February 2006.
2. Jim Hough, "Zoo Fund Reaches $108,200," *Lansing State Journal,* 2 October 1972, p. 1A.
3. Jim Hough, "Lansing's Potter Park Zoo Rated Outstanding for City Our Size," *Lansing State Journal,* 15 August 1976, "Welcome to Lansing: A Newcomers Guide to the Area," p. 96.
4. Bill Swix, interviewed by Kevin Hile, 25 February 2006. Subsequent quotes by Swix are also from this interview.
5. Ellen and Sonny Lumbert, interviewed by Kevin Hile, 1 February 2006.
6. Mary Anne McNamara, interviewed by Kevin Hile, 1 February 2006.

CHAPTER 4

1. Jim Hough, "Bingo a Real Cutie," *Lansing State Journal,* 9 November 1972, p. 1.
2. Bruce Snyder, interviewed by Kevin Hile, 27 February 2006.
3. Mike Hughes, "Potter Park Zoo Woes Worry City," *Lansing State Journal,* 17 October 1974, p. 6B.

4. Jim Hough, "The Onlooker," *Lansing State Journal,* 7 July 1975, p. 1B.
5. Dan Poorman, "Zoo Keeper Defending Bingo's Chains," *Lansing State Journal,* 3 September 1974, pp. 4-5B.
6. Dr. Jim Sikarskie, interviewed by Kevin Hile, 13 February 2006.
7. Mark Nixon, "Bingo Succumbs, Causes Unknown," *Lansing State Journal,* 14 August 1979, pp. 1A, 3A.
8. Amy C. Schumacher, "Your Opinion: Was Bingo Happy Cooped Up in the Zoo?," *Lansing State Journal,* 25 August, 1979, p. 6A.
9. Jan Martin Brigham, "Point of View: Don't Equate Man with Animal," *Lansing State Journal,* 24 September 1979, p. 8A.
10. Jim Hough, "The Onlooker," *Lansing State Journal,* 9 September 1979, p. 1B.
11. Jan Brigham, in an e-mail to Kevin Hile, 17 August 2006.
12. Jim Hough, "Welcome to Zoo, Tombi," *Lansing State Journal,* 9 November 1979, p. 1B.
13. Doug Finley, "Tombi Needs to Live in Herd Atmosphere," *Lansing State Journal,* 10 September 1989, p. 13A.
14. Doug Finley, interviewed by Kevin Hile, 7 February 2006.
15. John Schneider, "Tombi's Timid, but Pursuing an Artistic Career," *Lansing State Journal,* 28 February 1992, p. 1B.

CHAPTER 5

1. Mike Hughes, "Potter Park Vandalism Example of Trend," *Lansing State Journal,* 8 January 1977, pp. 1A, 3A.
2. Ibid.
3. Jim Hough, "This Bird Cage Is Special," *Lansing State Journal,* 5 August 1981, pp. 1-2B.
4. Kathy Barks Hoffman, "Vote for Potter Park Zoo Bonds Surprises 'Friends,'" *Lansing State Journal,* 8 August 1984, p. 3A.
5. Doug Finley, interviewed by Kevin Hile, 7 February 2006.
6. Leona Ison, "Spectators Turn Out to Welcome Penguins," *Lansing State Journal,* 20 July 1986, pp. 1B, 3B.
7. Bruce Snyder, interviewed by Kevin Hile, 27 February 2006.
8. Jim Hough, "The Onlooker: Pete and Friends Will Strut at Zoo Parade," *Lansing State Journal,* 17 July 1986, p. 1B.
9. Jim Hough: 'The Onlooker: Potter Park Zoo Day Mixes Excitement, a Touch of Sadness," *Lansing State Journal,* 22 July 1986, p. 1B.

CHAPTER 6

1. "Broadcast Pioneer Aids Zoo Lions," *Lansing State Journal,* 30 June 1987, p. 1A.
2. Ellen and Sonny Lumbert, interviewed by Kevin Hile, 1 February 2006.
3. "Animals' Best Friends," *Lansing State Journal,* 19 July 1988, pp. 1D, 4D.
4. Ibid.
5. Doug Finley, interviewed by Kevin Hile, 7 February 2006. Subsequent quotes from Finley are also from this interview.
6. Judi Corr, interviewed by Kevin Hile, 19 January 2008. Subsequent quotes from Corr are from this interview.
7. Carol Webster, interviewed by Kevin Hile, 4 April 2006. Subsequent quotes from Webster are from this interview.
8. Gerry Brady, interviewed by Kevin Hile, 12 May 2006. Subsequent quotes from Brady are from this interview.
9. Unfortunately, Bear Country owners were suspected by AZA officials of selling some of their grizzly bears for unlawful purposes. The story was later reported by local station WCCO-TV. See "Rapid City Owners Accused of Selling Grizzly Parts," http://wcco.com/crime/local_story_168143349.html, 17 June 2006. Potter Park Zoo stopped dealing with Bear Country years before this story broke in the media.
10. Michael W. Fox, *Inhumane Society: The American Way of Exploiting Animals* (New York: St. Martin's Press, 1990).
11. Alan Green, *Animal Underground: Inside America's Black Market for Rare and Exotic Species* (New York: Public Affairs, 1999).
12. Sheila Schimpf, "Zoo Fee Will Signal Beginning of the End," *Lansing State Journal,* 23 August 1991, p. 1D.
13. Dolores Maidlow-Kramer, "Points of View: Fenner Arboretum Good Home for Elvis," *Lansing State Journal,* 13 January 1995, p. 9A.
14. Dr. Jim Sikarskie, interviewed by Kevin Hile, 13 February 2006.
15. Jan Brigham, interviewed by Kevin Hile, 9 February 2006.

CHAPTER 7

1. Mary Anne McNamara, interviewed by Kevin Hile, 1 February 2006. Subsequent quotes from McNamara are also from this interview.

2. Gerry Brady, interviewed by Kevin Hile, conducted 11, 12, and 17 May 2006.
3. "Wild Jobs with Wildlife," *Occupational Outlook Quarterly,* spring 2001, p. 5. This report is released by the U.S. Bureau of Labor Statistics, which does not keep separate statistics for the occupation of zoo keeper, but rather groups keepers with other similar occupations.
4. Jan Brigham, interviewed by Kevin Hile, 9 February 2006.
5. John Schneider, "Camel Crush," *Lansing State Journal,* 22 May 1997, p. 1B
6. Jan Brigham, interviewed by Kevin Hile, 9 February 2006.
7. Bill Swix, interviewed by Kevin Hile, 25 February 2006.
8. Kimberly M. Gaudin, "An Incredible Fox Tale," *Lansing State Journal,* 7 April 1990, p. 1A.
9. Emmet Berg, "Tiger Brothers Had Slingshots," *New York Post,* 1 January 2008, cited from http://www.nypost.com/seven/01012008/news/nationalnews/tiger_brothers_had_slingshots_480170.htm.
10. Jan Brigham, in an email to Kevin Hile, 28 August 2006.

CHAPTER 8

1. Alister Doyle, "Humans Spur Worst Extinctions since Dinosaurs," accessed on *Planet Ark* Web site, http://www.planetark.com/dailynewsstory.cfm/newsid/35734/story.htm, 21 March 2006.
2. Dr. Duane Ullrey, interviewed by Kevin Hile, 12 June 2006. Subsequent quotes are also from this interview.
3. Dr. Tara Myers Harrison, interviewed by Kevin Hile, 18 May 2006. Subsequent quotes from Dr. Harrison are also from this interview.

CHAPTER 9

1. Dr. Jim Sikarskie, interviewed by Kevin Hile, 13 February 2006.
2. Bill Swix, in a letter to Kevin Hile, 17 August 2006
3. Ina Martin, interviewed by Kevin Hile, 3 May 2006
4. Kelliann Whitney, interviewed by Kevin Hile, 11 June 2006. Subsequent quotes from Whitney are also from this interview.

5. Dennis Laidler, interviewed by Kevin Hile, 20 June 2006. Subsequent quotes from Laidler are also from this interview.
6. Diane McNeil, interviewed by Kevin Hile, 15 May 2006.

CHAPTER 10

1. Eric Reickel, interviewed by Kevin Hile, 1 June 2006. Subsequent quotes from Reickel are also from this interview.
2. Tim Makinen, "Zoological Society Look at Turnover Proposal," *Lansing State Journal,* 27 March 1991, p. 1B.
3. Yvette Lanier, "Zoo Staff Stunned by Death of Spike, a Rare Rhino," *Lansing State Journal,* 9 February 2008, p. B1.
4. Karlene Rabidoux, "Council Dithers on Wine, Beer Plan," *Lansing State Journal,* 8 July 2000, p. 9A.
5. Sally Tato, "Serving Alcohol at Zoo Debated," *Lansing State Journal,* 16 April 2000, p. 3B.
6. Diane McNeil, interviewed by Kevin Hile, 15 May 2006. Subsequent quotes from McNeil are also from this interview.
7. Tom Lambert, "City May Dip into Parks Millage for Zoo," *Lansing State Journal,* 29 April 2006, p. 1B. Mayor Virg Bernero wanted $195,000 from the parks millage to be used for zoo operations.
8. Murdock Jemerson, interviewed by Kevin Hile, 1 June 2006.
9. Jim Hough, interview with Kevin Hile, 4 February 2006.

About the Author

Photo by Jim Fordyce.

Kevin Hile has been a docent at Potter Park Zoo since 1999. Before that, he volunteered at the Detroit Zoo for three years. Kevin graduated from Adrian College in 1988 and married his college sweetheart, Janet, that year. After working in a gloomy plastics factory in Ohio for almost a year after graduation, he became an assistant editor for reference book publisher Gale Research in Detroit. Here he rose to the position of senior editor before moving to Mason in 1998 and working for American Collegiate Marketing in Okemos. He went freelance in 2001, and in 2007 began work as a Web site designer and publications manager for the Lansing-based company Media Matters of Michigan, which is owned by entertainment reporter Jim Fordyce.

Kevin is the author of several nonfiction titles for children and young adults, including *Animal Rights, The Trial of Juveniles as Adults, Centaurs, Cesar Chavez, Ghost Ships,* and *Dams & Levees,* as well as the fantasy novel *The Steel of Enadia.* Upcoming books by Kevin include *The Handy Weather Answer Book,* 2nd edition, and a possible collaboration with Jim Fordyce about entertainers who were born in Michigan. Of all these accomplishments, however, Kevin is most proud of *Little Zoo by the Red Cedar* and of recording Potter Park Zoo's history before any more of its past is forgotten.

Breinigsville, PA USA
18 November 2010

249528BV00003B/185/P

9 781606 930625